"Boyd and Eddy present a compelling case that the Gospels were composed using eyewitness accounts passed down from the earliest followers of Jesus. This volume should be read by anyone interested in the ongoing discussion of the reliability of the Gospels and the truth about the historical Jesus."

Mark L. Strauss, professor of New Testament,
Bethel Seminary San Diego

"It is never easy to speak clearly and concisely about complex matters such as the historical Jesus and the evidence for the character and reality of his existence, but Greg Boyd and Paul Rhodes Eddy clearly have the gift for such communication without in any way trivializing the subject. They take the approach of teasing the audience's mind into active thought, not reducing a profound subject to *pablum*.

"Building on their more scholarly work on this same subject (*The Jesus Legend*), *Lord or Legend?* now provides us with a user-friendly guide on the subject of the historical reliability of the Gospels and the portraits they present us of Jesus, directed to the educated lay person. Taking on a lot of nonsense that passes for knowledge nowadays, Boyd and Eddy do not shy away from the tough historical, cultural, textual, and logical questions and their implications. Both those of a modernist and those of a postmodernist bent will find this a helpful clarification of issues relating to the truth about the historical Jesus. As it turns out, recent claims that Jesus wasn't and did not claim to be the Lord aren't historical—they're purely legendary!"

Ben Witherington III, professor of New Testament,
Asbury Theological Seminary

"Under a single cover, Greg Boyd and Paul Eddy provide a potpourri of gems. Both addressing the critical scholars who downgrade the data for the historical Jesus, as well as defending the historicity of the Gospels, this accessible reference tool provides an overview that answers many of the major criticisms that circulate in both scholarship as well as in the popular media. Some of the issues included here are rarely treated elsewhere. Altogether, the impact of this book is to equip the searching student with plenty of reasons to defend their faith. Congratulations, Baker Books, for continuing your fine tradition of publishing books that provide intellectual grist."

Gary R. Habermas, distinguished research professor and chair,
department of philosophy and theology, Liberty University.

Also by Gregory A. Boyd and Paul Rhodes Eddy

LORD OR LEGEND?

Wrestling with the Jesus Dilemma

Gregory A. Boyd
and Paul Rhodes Eddy

BakerBooks
Grand Rapids, Michigan

Published by Baker Books
a division of Baker Publishing Group
P.O. Box 6287, Grand Rapids, MI 49516-6287
www.bakerbooks.com

Printed in the United States of America

Library of Congress Cataloging-in-Publication Data
Boyd, Gregory A., 1957–
    Lord or legend? : wrestling with the Jesus dilemma / Gregory A. Boyd and Paul Rhodes Eddy.
        p.   cm.
    Includes bibliographical references (p.   ) and indexes.
    ISBN 10: 0-8010-6505-4 (pbk.)
    ISBN 978-0-8010-6505-7 (pbk.)
    1. Apologetics. 2. Jesus Christ—Historicity. 3. Bible—Evidences, authority, etc.
I. Eddy, Paul R. II. Title.
BT1103.B69 2007
232.9'08—dc22   2007018844

We dedicate this book to our siblings:

Debbie Sparrow, Anita Prosser, and Chris Boyd,
with fond childhood memories and heartfelt love,
Greg

and

Robert W. Eddy,
my brother and my friend,
I love and appreciate you, bro
(L.T. dude),
Paul

Contents

Acknowledgments

We want to thank our Baker editor, Robert Hosack, for encouraging us to write this book and for his unending encouragement (and patience) through the process. For over ten years we have enjoyed working with Bob on a number of projects—he is an amazing editor and a true friend.

Thanks also go to a number of people whose input on our larger work, *The Jesus Legend*, has also served to influence this shorter work: James Beilby, Michael Holmes, Erik Leafblad, Jeff Lehn, and Stewart Kelly. Our appreciation also goes to Betty Bond and the Bethel University Interlibrary Loan staff for their tireless help in tracking down countless volumes for us.

We are grateful for the support of our ecclesial family at Woodland Hills Church in St. Paul, Minnesota. We especially want to thank our fellow executive team member, Janice Rohling, for her support of—and patience with—our theological endeavors.

We want to thank our families—and especially our wives, Shelley Boyd and Kelly Eddy—for their unending support of our academic ventures. Finally, we want to acknowledge our siblings—Debbie Sparrow, Anita Prosser, Chris Boyd, and Robert Eddy—to whom we dedicate this book.

Introduction

The Jesus of History and the Challenge of Faith

he Challenge of Faith: We would like to start with a confession or two. The authors of this work are both Christian. Thus, with respect to the question of worldview, we both embrace Christian theism—but not always comfortably so. In terms of full-time vocation, one of us (Greg) is the senior pastor of a local church; the other (Paul) is a professor of theology at a Christian university. Nonetheless, *intellectually speaking*, faith has not always come easily for us. In fact, at different times in our lives, we have each found ourselves seriously questioning aspects of our Christian worldview. In these times, the question forces itself: Why did I ever find this belief to be credible?

Let those who are entirely without doubt cast the first stone! It strikes us that if what Christians believe about Jesus is rooted in reality and not wishful imagination, allowing one's faith to squarely face the difficult questions can't be a bad thing. Why should truth ever fear critical examination? In fact, critical examination of one's belief system is the only recipe we know to prevent self-delusion or unthinking, cultic fanaticism. Nor should anyone find it surprising that a Christian pastor and a Christian professor occasionally find themselves facing troubling questions about their Christian beliefs. Think about it! We are asked to believe that the Creator of the universe became a human by being born to a virgin, complete with an angelic chorus announcing his arrival. We're asked to believe that this man healed the sick, gave sight to the blind, made the lame walk, cured lepers, walked on water, turned water into wine, and multiplied food to feed thousands. Most shockingly, we're asked to believe both that this man was the long-awaited Jewish Messiah—the very embodiment of God—and that he died on a first-century Roman cross and then rose from the dead! One might ask, "How can any thinking person find it easy to accept such claims?"

The Jesus Dilemma: Factual History or Fictional Legend? Several decades ago, C. S. Lewis posed his now-famous "Jesus trilemma": "You must make your choice. Either this man was, and is, the Son of God: or else a madman or something worse. You can shut Him up for a fool, you can spit at him and kill him as a demon; or you can fall at his feet and call him Lord and God."[1] Some have pointed out, however, that this trilemma works only if Jesus actually made the sort of claims about himself recorded in the New Testament Gospels. In other words, before one can legitimately consider Lewis's *trilemma*, one must first wrestle with a prior *dilemma*: Is the basic portrait of Jesus offered in the Gospels a faithful reflection of the Jesus of history? Or is it largely a legendary fabrication spun out of the imaginations of the early Christians?

For many people in our contemporary, Western culture, it is a lot easier to accept that the portrait(s) of Jesus found in the Gospels is *legendary* than it is to accept that it is *historical*.[2] After all, when most people read similar stories—stories that include reports of the supernatural—about other religious figures (Krishna, Buddha, etc.), they generally assume the story is largely, if not entirely, a fictitious legend. The question then is naturally raised: Why should anyone think things are different with the story of Jesus?

But here is the interesting thing—and this is really what this book is about. As we have seriously asked ourselves this question again and again over the years, the authors of this book have found ourselves coming back to the conclusion that *the Jesus story is different!* While it is possible to explain many of the miraculous exploits of other religious figures as mere legends, we have found it very difficult to explain the Jesus story this way. Yes, we confess the story itself can initially seem implausible. But we have found that, if you honestly examine all the evidence, trying to explain the story as merely legendary is *even more* implausible.

In all honesty, a main reason the authors of this book continue to profess faith in Jesus is because we cannot with integrity account for the evidence without concluding that the Gospel presentation of Jesus is deeply rooted in history. Of course, our faith is not *entirely* based on historical evidence. As we shall explain in chapter 12, our faith, like everyone else's faith (whatever its object), is also rooted in personal experience and deep intuitions of the heart. Still, if the Jesus story wasn't as solidly rooted in history as we've found it to be, we would, in all likelihood, still believe the Jesus story is the most *beautiful* legend ever told—but we wouldn't base our lives on the conviction that the story *actually happened*. This book was written to share with lay readers why its authors have repeatedly come to this conclusion. But before we begin to set forth our case, we need to make five preliminary comments that will set the stage for our project.

1. *Our thesis.* As the title of this book suggests, we are interested in whether the historical evidence supports the conclusion that the portrayal of the earthly Jesus found in the New Testament Gospels is historically accurate or whether it supports viewing this portrayal mostly as a fictional legend. *Our thesis is that, if considered with an open mind, the evidence strongly supports the conclusion that the portrayal of Jesus within the Gospels is historically accurate.*

To be more specific, our thesis is that, if one remains genuinely open to the historical *possibility* that the Gospels' portrait of Jesus is generally reliable—that is, if one doesn't assume at the start that the story can't be reliable—one will find many compelling reasons for concluding that this portrait of Jesus is the *most historically probable* understanding available. In addition, we believe that the historical evidence is such that it can serve as a central part of the intellectual basis that warrants a person going on to accept the Gospels' claim that Jesus is the saving Son of God and to commit his or her life to him as Lord.

2. *What we are* not *doing.* Second, and closely related to our first point, it is important for readers to notice that we are only claiming the evidence demonstrates that it is *more probable than not* that the Gospels' portrait of Jesus is rooted in history, and thus that it is not merely legendary. We are *not* claiming the historical evidence *proves with absolute certainty* that *every* aspect of the Gospels' portrait of Jesus is historically accurate. And we certainly are not claiming the historical evidence can *prove* that Jesus is the divine and sovereign Lord of all. This might leave some readers

disappointed. They might have hoped that we were going to prove the Gospels are 100 percent historically accurate, that Jesus is Lord, and, perhaps, that the Gospels are divinely inspired.

But you see, no one can *prove* these sorts of things on strictly historical grounds. By its very nature, historical research can only offer conclusions of *probability*—never *certainty*. This is the case because, however strong a historical argument is, no one can travel back into the past to verify with *certainty* its historical claim. For example, although virtually everyone agrees that Julius Caesar crossed the Rubicon, Hannibal crossed the Alps, and George Washington crossed the Delaware, each of these historical claims is a matter of probability—not absolute certainty. Thus, because of the existence of historically possible alternative scenarios and the impossibility of time-travel, historians can only make claims at the level of probabilities. To be frank, anyone who claims to be able to "prove with absolute certainty" a historical claim has forgotten the inherent limitations of the historical enterprise and the finite and always fallible nature of human knowledge.

Additionally, historical research alone cannot *prove* articles of faith (e.g., "Jesus is Lord," or "the Gospels are divinely inspired"). This is why they are called articles *of faith*. The most that historical research can do is to demonstrate that having faith in these matters is—or is not—*reasonable*. To put the matter simply: Although we are both Christian theologians by training, in this book we are involved in *an exercise in historical inquiry, not Christian theology*. Thus, in this book we will not directly be considering theological articles of faith such as the claims that the Gospels are divinely inspired or the claim that Jesus is the divine Lord of all. However, we are convinced that the conclusions of our historical project in this book do have a direct bearing upon such theological questions. Specifically, we believe that the historical evidence plays an important role in demonstrating that placing one's faith in Jesus as Lord—that is, Jesus as he is presented in the Gospels—is an appropriately *reasonable* response.

3. *The "Legendary-Jesus Theory."* Throughout this work we shall be engaging a certain scholarly perspective we label the "legendary-Jesus theory." With this label we are not only, or even primarily, referring to the small minority of radical scholars who believe the Jesus story is *entirely* a legend (or myth), though the label certainly includes them.[3] Rather, we are primarily referring to scholars who hold that the portrait of Jesus in the Gospels is *substantially* legendary—hence *not* substantially rooted in

history. More precisely, we include in this group all who conclude that the substance of the Gospels' witness to Jesus making divine claims, doing supernatural deeds, and rising from the dead is *legendary*. Our goal is to demonstrate that historical evidence does not support this view. It rather supports the view that it is more likely than not that these and other aspects of the Gospel story are rooted in history.

4. *Our intended audience.* We have written this book for critically minded laypeople. We believe the material we will be reviewing is much too important to be kept within the walls of academic scholarship. For some, we hope this book will provide a solid intellectual foundation to the faith they already embrace. For others, we hope this book will compel them seriously to consider accepting that the Jesus story is rooted in history and thus to consider accepting the Gospels' theological interpretation that Jesus is Lord and, subsequently, to commit themselves to following him.

In any case, we have written this book for the interested layperson and have thus attempted to keep it as brief and as readable as possible without overly compromising the quality of the scholarship. If some readers desire to explore certain issues raised here in a more thorough manner, we encourage them to consult our more academic (and much longer!) coauthored book, *The Jesus Legend: A Case for the Historical Reliability of the Synoptic Jesus Tradition.*[4]

5. *The outline of this book.* Finally, it may help for readers to have a general sense of how our argument will unfold. We divide our work into two parts. In part 1, "Jesus, History, and Legend-Making," we evaluate an assortment of arguments legendary-Jesus theorists put forth to make their case that the Jesus story found in the Gospels is not solidly rooted in history. Some of the questions we'll be addressing in this section are

- Must a historian using the historical-critical method assume that all reports of supernatural occurrences are legendary? That is, is a critical historian ever warranted in drawing the conclusion that it's more probable than not that a report of supernatural occurrences is rooted in history?

- Was first-century Palestine an environment that was conducive to the evolution of a legend about a miracle-working God-man?

- Is the Jesus story unique, or is it significantly similar to various myths and legends we find in history?

- What do we make of the (alleged) silence about the earthly Jesus in Paul's letters, which were written before the Gospels?
- The Jesus story circulated primarily in oral form for decades before the Gospels were written. But how well are oral traditions able to preserve historical material over such a time period?

In part 2, "The Gospels and Ten Tests of Historical Reliability," we sharpen our focus on the Gospels themselves. Treating the Gospels the same as we would any other ancient writing, we apply ten criteria historians customarily use to evaluate the historical reliability of ancient documents. One distinctive aspect of our assessment is the conviction that recent findings by scholars who study orally oriented cultures have a significant bearing on our estimation of how the Gospels stand up to critical scrutiny. Hence, we shall weave findings from "orality studies" into our application of the ten questions historians typically ask of ancient documents. These questions are

1. Do we possess copies of the ancient work that are reasonably close to the original?
2. Did the work intend to communicate reliable history, or was it intended to be read as fiction?
3. Was the author of the work in a position to record the history he or she claims to report?
4. How much did the biases of the author affect his or her historical reporting?
5. Do the works include the kind of detail that tends to accompany reports that are rooted in eyewitness testimony?
6. Does the work incorporate material that is "self-damaging"—that is, material that works counter to any bias the author seems to have, and thus material one might have expected the writer to leave out?
7. Is the work self-consistent or consistent with other works that report on the same events?
8. Are the events recorded intrinsically believable or unbelievable?
9. Is there any other literary evidence that impacts our assessment of the document under examination?
10. Are there any archaeological findings that either confirm or undermine the claims made by the document under examination?

Following this, we will conclude our book by exploring the relationship the Jesus story has to legend and myth in general. Paradoxically, though we'll spend the entire book arguing that the Jesus story cannot plausibly be regarded as a legend or myth, in chapter 12 we'll argue that there is an important sense in which this story constitutes the very essence of myth. Indeed, we'll argue that discovering the "mythic" quality of the Jesus story serves to further confirm its historicity.

Our hope is that this book informs readers about the current state of scholarship on issues surrounding the historicity of the Gospels' Jesus story while demonstrating the case for accepting this story as substantially historical, not legendary. In this way we hope to persuade some readers of the reasonableness of placing their faith in Jesus Christ as Lord.

PART ONE

Jesus, History, and Legend-Making

I n part 1 we critically assess several major arguments legendary-Jesus theorists put forth in support of their claim that the Gospels' portrait of Jesus is substantially legendary. Perhaps the most fundamental reason many scholars conclude that the Gospels' portrait of Jesus is mostly, if not entirely, legendary is that it depicts Jesus as performing supernatural feats. Legendary-Jesus theorists generally assume that supernatural events do not occur and thus assume that any writings that contain accounts of supernatural occurrences must be, by definition, either myth or legend. In chapter 1 we consider the widespread assumption within Western academic circles that supernatural events do not—in fact, cannot—occur.

Myths and legends typically are created to express certain cultural convictions and meet certain social needs. This is why the process of legend-making can almost always be explained sociologically. The question is, Can the Gospels' portrait of Jesus as a miracle-working divine man most plausibly be explained in this way?

Some legendary-Jesus theorists argue that first-century Judaism had come under the influence of the surrounding Hellenistic (Greek-influenced) pagan culture to such a degree that it would be natural for a legend of this sort to arise. Thus, they assert that this story can be explained purely sociologically—that is, without supposing that Jesus *actually* made the divine claims or did the supernatural deeds the Gospels attribute to him. We will consider this claim in chapter 2.

Another major line of argumentation put forth by some legendary-Jesus theorists—particularly by those who hold that the story has no foundation in history whatsoever—is that little if any historical information about Jesus can be found in the letters of Paul (which were written prior to the Gospels). In fact, some scholars maintain that Paul didn't even think of Jesus as a recent, historical figure. Rather, he viewed Jesus as a cosmic figure who redeemed the world in the celestial realms or in the distant past. In chapter 3 we will examine the case these scholars make for a mythic or legendary Christ on this basis.

Another common reason given for viewing the Jesus of the Gospels as substantially legendary is that the story about Jesus parallels other myths and legendary tales. Myths about dying and rising gods were common in the ancient world, it is claimed. Legends about heroes who were born of a virgin, were almost killed in early childhood, and so on, have been common throughout history. And history affords us other examples of charismatic individuals who purportedly performed miracles and gained a following of worshippers. In chapter 4, therefore, we will examine the argument that these parallels provide evidence that the Jesus story is not unique and thus should be considered mostly, if not entirely, legendary.

Finally, virtually all scholars agree that material about Jesus primarily circulated by word of mouth among the early Christian communities prior to the writing of the Gospels. Those who hold that the Gospels' portrait of Jesus is substantially legendary uniformly hold that these oral traditions were very unreliable. Hence, it is claimed, the Jesus story was progressively distorted as the early Christians added fictional elements while telling and retelling it. Drawing on a wealth of findings from various disciplines concerned with orality studies over the last several decades, we shall assess this perspective on oral traditions in chapter 5.

1

Miraculous Claims
and the Critical Mind

Can Intelligent People
Still Believe in the Supernatural?

The Gospels present Jesus as making divine claims, performing incredible miracles, and rising from the dead.[1] According to the New Testament, this is what convinced the earliest Jewish disciples that he was the Son of God. But this is also the most fundamental reason many contemporary New Testament scholars, as well as others, find it hard to accept that the Gospels are historically reliable. We in the Western world have all been influenced by the naturalistic worldview that arose out of the scientific revolution and the intellectual Enlightenment that followed. The naturalistic worldview holds that everything that happens can in principle be explained by appealing to laws of nature. Miracles, therefore, are ruled out of court. To the extent that we've been influenced by this worldview, we intuitively find it difficult to accept as factual reports that contain miracles. We're inclined to dismiss them as legends.

A good percentage of New Testament scholars today accept this naturalistic worldview, which is why so much of contemporary New Testament scholarship is spent trying to explain in naturalistic terms how the portrait of Jesus as a supernatural figure found in the Gospels came into being. Burton Mack expresses the firm conviction of many when he writes, "The emergence of Christianity and its literature can be understood without recourse or caveats with regard to miracles, resurrections, divine appearances, presences, or unusual charismatic phenomena."[2] So too, Robert Funk, the founder of the famous (or infamous) Jesus Seminar, argues that "the notion that God interferes with the order of nature . . . is no longer credible. . . . Miracles . . . contradict the regularity of the order of the physical universe. . . . God does not interfere with the laws of nature." Given this assumption, he has no choice but to contend that "the resurrection of Jesus did not involve the resuscitation of a corpse. Jesus did not rise from the dead, except perhaps in some metaphorical sense."[3]

John Dominic Crossan agrees when he concludes his discussion of the biblical account of Jesus raising Lazarus from the dead by saying, "I do not think this event ever did or could happen. . . . I do not think that anyone, anywhere, at any time brings dead people back to life."[4] In short, these aspects of the Jesus story may be mythologically true—that is, true in the sense that they express longings and intuitions of the human heart—but they cannot be accepted as *historically* true. The assumption of naturalism rules this option out, and it lies at the heart of the legendary-Jesus hypothesis.

As we shall see throughout this book, providing a plausible naturalistic explanation for how some of the specific supernatural aspects of the portrait of Jesus found in the Gospels came into being is no easy endeavor. But before we examine these attempts, we need to critically assess the assumption of naturalism that drives them. There are at least five objections that can be raised against this assumption.

An Unwarranted Assumption

First, while every modern person of course grants that the world generally runs in accordance with natural laws, on what basis can anyone argue that it does so *exhaustively*—that is, without there ever being exceptions to these so-called laws? The absolute rejection of miracles isn't really a *conclusion* that is based on evidence or on reason—for neither evidence nor reason could warrant such an absolute conclusion. It is, rather, an *assumption*—a presupposition of the naturalistic worldview—pure and simple.

Holding to this or any other assumption in an uncritical, dogmatic manner doesn't coincide well with a critical, open-minded enterprise. As the great philosopher of history R. G. Collingwood argued, to the extent that one's research and findings are rooted in a priori dogmatic assumptions, such research can't be considered critical (or, in his terms, "scientific") scholarship.[5] More specifically, the goal of scholarly historical-critical research is to draw probabilistic conclusions on the basis of evidence, not assume certain conclusions (such as, "*everything* can be explained in natural terms") prior to an open investigation of the evidence.

Of course, since we all agree that events *generally* happen in accordance with natural laws, it makes sense to *prefer* naturalistic explanations over supernatural ones, all other things being equal. But this is quite different from assuming at the outset that *all* events *must* be explained in naturalistic terms. A more open-minded, scholarly approach would be to hold that, if all available natural explanations become implausible, we should consider explanations that go beyond the known natural laws that describe how the world generally operates.

The "Laws" of Nature

Second, as we saw above, naturalism holds that everything can be explained by appealing to natural laws. Framing the issue in terms of "laws" has given some the impression that they are rules nature *must* obey—which is in part why many scholars conclude that miracles are impossible. Our second objection to this naturalistic perspective, however, is that this understanding of the laws of nature goes beyond anything science can determine. A natural law is a *description* of what we *generally* find in the world, not a *prescription* for what we *must* find in the world. Hence, while a supernatural event is an exception to the regular operations of nature, it does not violate an inviolable law of nature, as some maintain.

This point is especially relevant in light of twentieth-century scientific advances, for throughout the last century we have discovered that the supposed laws of nature are generally *probabilistic*. For example, quantum physics has taught us that there is an element of randomness pervading everything at a subatomic level. We can describe the behavior of quantum particles (or waves) in general terms, according to Schrödinger's equation. But, as a matter of principle, we cannot predict exactly how any given particle will behave.[6]

Among other things, this means that the solidity of the things we experience every day (e.g., the book you're reading, the chair you're sitting on, the hand that holds up the book) is probabilistic. As a matter of fact, the book, chair, and hand are actually losing and acquiring particles every moment. It's just that our sensory faculties can't detect this subatomic activity. If the majority of quantum particles of the book, chair, or hand randomly acted at the extremity of their possible behavior—that is, their least probable but still possible behavior—the book, chair, or hand would completely disintegrate. Fortunately, while the behavior of single particles embodies an element of randomness, the behavior of large groups of particles is very predictable. And so, you needn't worry about anything spontaneously disintegrating.

Our point is that we now know the world runs on probability. What we call "laws of nature" are simply descriptions of maximally probable behavior. And in this light we can see how unwarranted it is to claim that the laws of nature rule out the possibility of extraordinary events—including miracles.

The Principle of Analogy

The naturalistic approach to history has been buttressed in academic circles by what has come to be known as "the principle of analogy."[7] The basic idea is that all understanding—whether it be of people's behavior or of natural events—is rooted in analogies drawn from our own experience. What bears no analogy with our own experience is utterly incomprehensible to us. So, the reasoning goes, our understanding of the past must be by analogy with our experience of the present. And since (it has been assumed) we have no experience of the supernatural in the present, we must of necessity try to understand all aspects of history without appealing to the supernatural. Our third objection to the anti-supernaturalism of the naturalistic worldview is that the argument against the possibility of miracles on the basis of the principle of analogy is seriously flawed. Consider two arguments.

1. Even if, for the moment, we grant that modern people never experience miracles, it doesn't at all follow that we can't analogically understand what a miracle would be like. Among other things, a miracle is an event that has a nonphysical cause. What's so difficult about analogically understanding *this*?

Indeed, far from having no analogy in our present experience, it could be argued that we experience events with nonphysical causes every time we make a free decision. Some materialists may *believe* all free decisions are nothing more than physical effects of previous physical causes, but this is not how they—or any of us—*experience* our own free decisions. We experience our decisions as free precisely because we *don't* experience them as exhaustively determined by previous physical causes. We experience ourselves as free to the extent that we experience possibilities as being *up to us*—not antecedent physical causes—to resolve.

Regardless of what one believes about freedom, this experience of freedom provides an analogy for understanding what a miracle would be like, even if a person hasn't personally experienced one. And if we can analogically understand what a miracle would be like, we can conceivably confront evidence that would make it reasonable to conclude that one has in fact taken place.

2. If the principle of analogy were applied consistently the way it is applied when certain historians rule out the possibility of miracles, we'd have to conclude that people who rule out the possibility of anything sufficiently beyond their own experience are thinking reasonably. But this is clearly wrong. To illustrate, just because people who have lived for centuries in tropical rainforests have never experienced anything like snow, it doesn't follow that we should conclude they're thinking rationally (let alone critically and scientifically) if they concluded on this basis that snow doesn't exist!

Here again science provides an excellent illustration. No one has ever experienced anything that has both particle and wavelike properties. We can't picture such an entity. And yet, since the early twentieth century, physicists have had to accept—on the basis of evidence—that light has just these properties. Anyone today who would dismiss such claims because he or she has no analogy for such a thing in his or her own experience would not be regarded as thinking rationally. The point is, we must follow the evidence, even if it leads us to postulate things for which we have no clear analogy in our experience. Perhaps it's time we applied some of this insight to the way we think historically.

The Experience of the Supernatural Today

A fourth fundamental problem with the modern rejection of the possibility of miracles is that, while certain Western scholars may not experience miracles, many people in the West and around the globe *do*! Hence, while these scholars may (mistakenly) believe they have nothing in their experience to help them analogically understand a supernatural occurrence in the past, they cannot justify their claim that modern people in general have no analogy by which to understand supernatural occurrences. Step outside one slice of academic Western culture and you find that the world is full of reported experiences of the miraculous!

For example, throughout history and even today the phenomenon of demon possession and exorcism is quite common.[8] We find eyewitness reports of people levitating, things flying through the air on their own, bodies contorting in ways seemingly impossible to explain in natural terms, and the like. So too, throughout history and even today people have encountered (or at least are convinced they have encountered) angelic or demonic presences as well as healings and "coincidences" they believe to be supernaturally caused.[9]

In this light, it is clear that the claim that modern people don't experience the supernatural is simply wrong. What these scholars mean when they make such claims is that no one experiences anything *these scholars* would grant is supernatural. It is on this basis that they then argue that modern scholars can't admit the supernatural into their understanding of the past. But this is a clear case of circular reasoning. ("Circular reasoning" is where a conclusion is used as a premise to justify the conclusion.) These scholars *assume* that supernatural occurrences don't happen. On this basis they dismiss all present and past reports of supernatural occurrences. And from this they conclude that the world *always* operates according to natural laws. But notice, they only conclude this because they *presupposed* it at the start. If one doesn't presuppose supernatural

events never occur, and if one therefore takes reports of supernatural occurrences seriously, one will find there is plenty of evidence both in the
present and from the past that supernatural events do in fact occur.

An Example of Ethnocentrism

Finally, the rejection of the possibility of miracles is not only circular,
it's *ethnocentric*. That is, it is rooted in an assumption that a certain ethnic
perspective—namely, the modern, European, academic, naturalistic perspective—is superior to all others. A Western scholar could not as a matter
of principle dismiss the experience of the supernatural throughout history
and in most cultures even today unless he or she assumed at the start the
superiority of his or her own modern, naturalistic view of the world.

Interestingly enough, an increasing number of Western scholars in a
variety of fields are beginning to see the ethnocentric prejudice of this
dogmatic, naturalistic stance. Especially in the area of ethnography (the
study of ethnic groups), Western scholars are increasingly acknowledging
that their own naturalistic worldview has no right to claim superiority
over the worldviews of the people groups they're studying—almost all of
which allow for, and experience, supernatural occurrences.

Along these same lines, many ethnographers are now realizing that one
can only truly understand the worldview of a people group by viewing it,
and experiencing it, *from the inside*. So, for example, while Western ethnographers in the past have typically dismissed accounts of the supernatural
found in other cultures as being the result of their "primitive," unscientific
imagination, these scholars are now saying that Western scholars have
to take these accounts seriously and as potential challenges to their own
naturalistic assumptions.[10]

The results of this paradigm shift have been quite startling. Ethnographers are discovering that non-Western ways of looking at and experiencing the world often disclose aspects of reality missed by the naturalistic,
Western worldview.[11] Most significantly, a number of these specialists are
discovering for themselves that the supernatural is real![12]

It seems to us that those critical scholars who reject the possibility of
miracles carte blanche need to learn from these contemporary ethnographers and realize how ethnocentric their dogmatic anti-supernaturalistic

stance is. While many modern Western people may have trouble accepting the possibility of miracles, a truly critical scholarly approach should lead us humbly to concede that this difficulty may be nothing more than a liability and limitation of our own culturally shaped worldview. Rather than assume the superiority of our worldview, we should, when the evidence calls for it, allow the experience of other people in other cultures and at other times to call the absoluteness of our own worldview into question.

Conclusion

As noted above, we grant that, whether one is researching a past or a present occurrence, if it is possible to plausibly explain it in naturalistic terms, it *should* be explained in naturalistic terms. After all, the world does generally operate according to certain regular principles. What we deny, however, is that we should be dogmatically committed to naturalistic explanations, regardless of how implausible they become. If we remain aware that the laws of nature are descriptive and probabilistic and that the naturalistic worldview is as socially constructed as anyone else's, we may at some point encounter evidence that leads us to consider the possibility that something has occurred that can only be explained by appealing to supernatural forces.

Throughout the remainder of this book, we shall contend that the evidence surrounding the Jesus tradition is just such an instance. We shall argue that the purely naturalistic explanations given by certain scholars for the rise of this story are less plausible than the explanation the Gospel authors themselves provide—the supernatural elements included. If one remains genuinely open to the *possibility* that the Jesus story is generally rooted in history, we contend that they will discover the Jesus story is *most probably* rooted in history.

2

A Most Unexpected Legend

How Paganized Was First-Century Palestinian Judaism?

L egends are generally created to express certain social convictions and meet certain social needs. This is why the process of legend-making can almost always be explained sociologically. The question is, can the Gospels' portrait of Jesus as a miracle-working God-man be explained in this way? If it can be exhaustively explained by appealing to social convictions and needs present in the first-century Jewish Palestinian environment out of which it arose, then the legendary-Jesus thesis begins to gain in plausibility. If, however, we cannot easily explain the story in such a fashion, then we must seriously consider the possibility that it is rooted in actual historical events.[1]

We know that myths and legends about miracle-working gods interacting with humans, and even about humans becoming "divine," were quite common in the ancient Greco-Roman world, as they are in many other cultures. These stories expressed and reinforced the socio-religious-political beliefs and convictions of many Mediterranean peoples of the time. We also know that, beginning with Alexander the Great (fourth century BC), there was an intense effort on the part of Greco-Roman rulers to Hellenize (make Greek-like) all people groups under their authority. They wanted all of their subject nations to absorb Greek culture, religion, education, and so on.

Now, because they believed in the one Creator God, Jews typically resisted polytheistic, pagan stories about gods interacting with humans and/or humans becoming divine. In years past, this led many scholars to conclude that the location of the eventual paganization of Christianity could not have happened on Jewish soil. It was thought that as the Christian movement spread out from Palestine into the wider Mediterranean world, Gentile converts retained some of their polytheistic heritage, mixing it in a syncretistic fashion with the Judaism of the early Jesus movement. In this perspective, the idea that Jesus was divine is seen as a later paganized aberration of the original Jewish Jesus movement.

In recent years, however, this perspective has been seriously called into question. The reasons for this reassessment are several. First, the specific arguments of the alternative perspective in which an attempt was made to show early Christian borrowing of pagan religious ideas have now been shown to be seriously flawed. Second, the clear evidence of the *rapid speed* with which the worship of Jesus arose within the early Christian communities counts against the first view. In fact, it appears that we can trace the pattern of worshipping the risen Jesus as Yahweh-God back even to the first Palestinian Jewish followers of Jesus. Third, these Jewish followers were ardent monotheists, as the New Testament documents themselves clearly reveal (e.g., 1 Cor. 8:4; 1 Tim. 2:5). Larry Hurtado plainly summarizes the evidence:

> Both the chronological and the demographic data make it extremely dubious to attribute the level of devotion to Jesus that characterized earliest Christianity to syncretistic influences from the pagan religious context. Devotion to Jesus appears too early, and originated among circles of the early Jesus movement that were comprised of—or certainly dominated by—Jews, and they seem no more likely than other devout [monotheistic] Jews of the time to appropriate pagan religious influences.[2]

This recognition has led some legendary-Jesus theorists to take another look at first-century Judaism as a possible conduit for the paganization of early Christianity. After all, at this point in history, Palestine was ruled by Greek-influenced Roman rulers. Thus, some argue, we have good reason to conclude that the Jews of the first century may well have been Hellenized—even paganized—to the point where they, too, could have naturally imagined and disseminated a legend about a miracle-working divine man. Hence, some legendary-Jesus theorists argue that, while Jesus may (or may not) have existed and while aspects of the Jesus story may (or may not) be rooted in history, the religious claims of this story that seem to run counter to Jewish creational monotheism can be explained sociologically by appealing to the influence of the surrounding pagan environment upon Palestinian Judaism itself.

Evidence That First-Century Jews Were Significantly Hellenized

1. At Qumran on the Dead Sea, a library of works was discovered, most likely deriving from a Jewish group known as the Essenes. The library has come to be known as the Dead Sea Scrolls, and it dates to just before the time of Jesus. What is interesting for our purposes is that the library contains several magical/astrological texts—practices that were popular among non-Jews of the time but that were prohibited by the Jewish Scriptures. Some argue that this is proof that at least some Palestinian Jews around the time of Jesus had become significantly paganized.

2. A number of synagogues excavated in Palestine have been found decorated with zodiac symbols. For example, at Sepphoris a mosaic was discovered that depicts the god Dionysus riding a donkey, a depiction of Dionysus in a drinking contest with Heracles, and several bronze figurines, possibly of Pan and Prometheus, as well as a bull. These are definitely not things one would expect traditional, monotheistic Jews to have included in their synagogues! Similarly, an ancient synagogue unearthed at Tiberias, on the shores of the Sea of Galilee, had a floor mosaic of the Greek god Helios surrounded by a twelve-month zodiac wheel.[3] Some scholars argue these findings reveal the surprising extent to which Jews at the time of Jesus had absorbed Greco-Roman religious culture.

3. Some ancient Jewish literature just prior to the time of Jesus ascribes to certain angels and even humans attributes that were traditionally reserved for Yahweh alone. Some scholars argue that this suggests that Hellenism had "loosened up" the monotheism of the Jews of this time.

This loosening up can perhaps explain how first-century Jews could evolve a legend about a miracle-working divine man whom they came to worship as the embodiment of Yahweh.

4. Finally, some Jewish texts make references to certain people being divine, even calling them "divine men," just as many pagan texts do. To the thinking of some scholars, this reveals that there was a precedent for the early Christian practice of referring to Jesus as divine.[4]

On these grounds, many scholars argue that first-century Jewish culture provided a social environment that was as conducive for a legend about a miracle-working divine man as the broader Greco-Roman pagan culture. While later Jews would come to be appalled by a story of a divine man, let alone by the practice of praying to or worshipping this divine man, Jews around the time of Jesus were not—which is why it is possible to explain the Gospels' story of Jesus along purely sociologically motivated legendary lines.

Taking a Closer Look

We admit that the case for viewing first-century Jewish culture as significantly Hellenized looks rather impressive at first glance. In fact, with respect to a number of cultural aspects, it *was*! We shall argue, however, that when it came to *religious* matters, virtually all of the evidence suggests first-century Palestinian Jews as a whole vehemently resisted pagan influences. We will now consider each of the four pieces of evidence for a paganized first-century Judaism.

1. It is true that we have discovered magical and astrological texts among the Dead Sea Scrolls. This fact, however, does not necessarily mean the Essenes endorsed them. For example, it is certainly not the case that any given scholar today endorses all of the ideas in every book in his or her library! But even if the Essenes did endorse them, we need to bear in mind that the Qumran community was hardly representative of Jewish culture at large around the time of Jesus. They were an isolated, esoteric group who held a number of beliefs and practices other Jews rejected. More specifically, since magic and astrology were associated with fatalism in the ancient world, it may be that the Essenes used these texts to support their idiosyncratic views of predestination.

2. It is true that several Palestinian synagogues have been unearthed that contain pagan symbols. But it is also true that none of this evidence dates before the third century AD—and most of it derives from later than that.[5] As such, these findings tell us nothing about the beliefs and practices of Jews in the first century. Even apart from this, however, many scholars argue that these pagan symbols were likely devoid of religious significance, being used merely for decorative and calendar purposes.[6] Consider the fact that we in the West use a calendar that names days and months after pagan deities, but this hardly means we share the ancient religious faith in these pagan deities.

3. It is true that some religious texts prior to the time of Jesus occasionally refer to angels and humans in terms commonly used in connection with Yahweh. But it is also clear that in none of these texts is the creational-monotheistic line of distinction between the Creator and all other beings ever broached.

In this respect it is important to remember that ancient Jews never denied the existence of powerful "gods" (i.e., angelic beings) alongside Yahweh. The Old Testament is filled with references to heavenly beings, some of whom carry out Yahweh's will, others who fight against it. What defined Jewish orthodoxy, however, were the convictions that there is only one Creator God, no "god" is as powerful as the one true God, and no "god" should ever be worshiped other than the one true God. While the religious literature in the period leading up to the time of Christ occasionally exalts beings other than Yahweh, never do they compromise the traditional conviction that Yahweh alone is Creator, and never do they cross the line of advocating *worship* of these spiritual beings.[7] These texts thus provide no precedent for the remarkable way early Christians speak about and worship Jesus.

4. It is true that certain Jewish texts refer to "divine men." But, as Carl Holladay and others have demonstrated, it is also true that the Jewish use of this phrase was significantly different from its use in a pagan context. More specifically, Jews did not use this term to ascribe literal *divinity* to a person. It rather was used to refer to a godly person or to one whom God used in extraordinary ways.[8] As Holladay's meticulous research reveals, the Jews were repulsed by the notion that a human being could be, in any literal sense, divine—and thus a rival of Yahweh.[9]

Jewish Resistance to Hellenistic Religious Influences

We see that the case for viewing first-century Jewish culture as open to pagan religious ideas is not nearly as impressive as it may have first appeared. But it grows even weaker when we consider other evidence that the Jews of the first century tended to resist pagan religious ideas and remained true to their monotheistic tradition.

To begin, recent research suggests that the influence of Hellenism on most indigenous cultures under Greek and Roman rule was largely superficial. The pressure to conform to Hellenistic ideals often altered the *veneer* of indigenous cultures (e.g., architectural styles, entertainment, art, dress), but it rarely affected their traditional worldview or religious beliefs.[10] Indeed, in some instances, the influence of Hellenism actually seems to have *strengthened* the traditions and beliefs of these indigenous cultures.[11]

This seems to have been especially true of ancient Jews. In fact, some evidence indicates that Jews actually became *more* conservative in their monotheistic religious convictions *precisely because* they were surrounded by pagan culture. For example, Sardis was a thoroughly Hellenized city populated primarily by non-Jews. Yet, as A. T. Kraabel has established, all archaeological indications are that the Jews in this locale grew more strongly conservative precisely because they were surrounded by pagan culture.[12] Their disgust for the surrounding paganism apparently intensified their commitment to their monotheistic convictions.

There is some evidence that this strong resistance to Hellenism among Jews at Sardis was not uncommon. For example, we know that Roman emperors customarily excused Jews from the civilian obligation of worshipping national deities and being involved in national pagan religious activities. Moreover, they often printed special coins without the imprint of the emperor's face in regions heavily populated by Jews because these obviously monotheistic Jews regarded this as making a "graven image" (and thus violation of the second commandment), and it offended them. So too, throughout the Roman Empire, "Jews refused to honor gods, shrines, and cults other than their own."[13]

Such things clearly suggest that the Jews of the first century were holding fast to their monotheistic convictions. As a number of scholars have argued, it suggests that, at least as it concerns the Jewish *religion*, Hellenism did not influence first-century Jews in the direction of compromise; if anything, *it influenced them in the direction of deepening their convictions.*[14] Hence, according to these scholars, it is quite unlikely that first-century Jews would be inclined to accept elements of paganism or compromise their strict monotheism to any significant degree.[15]

The Intense Creational Monotheism of First-Century Palestinian Judaism

If this much is true of first-century Jews in general, it is even more characteristic of Palestinian Jews in particular—a point that is most significant inasmuch as this is the specific locale in which Christianity was birthed. The evidence that first-century Palestinian Jews remained strongly monotheistic and Torah-centered in their beliefs is overwhelming. Consider the following lines of evidence:

1. Josephus, who is our main literary source for first-century Judaism, depicts Palestinian Jews at this time as faithful to their traditional monotheistic beliefs and practices.[16]
2. In all of the archaeological sites in the Palestine area to date, pagan temples are completely absent![17]
3. Ceramic wares found in Galilee are carved from a distinctive soft chalk limestone. This type of vessel was held by Jews to meet ritual purity requirements and is found only in Jewish sites.[18]
4. A noticeable number of affluent Galilean homes contained a *miqwaoth* (ritual bathing pool), indicating that Jews continued to honor the practice of ritualistic bathing.[19]
5. In contrast to most pagan sites, Galilean excavation sites reveal a consistent lack of pork bones, indicating that the Jews of this locale honored the Levitical prohibition on eating pork.[20]
6. The burial sites in first-century Palestine are generally distinctly Jewish, allowing for bones to be collected and placed in a box (an ossuary) some time after the interment.[21]
7. Unearthed coins minted in Palestine in the first century tend to be free of visual representations, suggesting the Jews of this time were offended by "graven images"—hence, that they were deeply committed to following the Torah.[22]

It thus seems that, whatever influences Hellenism may have had upon the surface veneer of Jewish culture in Palestine, it did not in any noticeable manner affect their core religious convictions. The population as a whole remained "Torah-true in religious orientation."[23]

A Most Unexpected Myth

In light of these facts, it seems we cannot easily explain the creation of the Jesus story the way we typically explain the creation of pagan legends of the time. Indeed, far from expressing beliefs and meeting needs in their culture, as legends typically do, the Jesus story runs directly *counter* to certain fundamental aspects of its Jewish environment.

Most importantly, this story involves the claim that a man—a contemporary man no less—*is to be worshipped as God*. Nothing could have been more antithetical to first-century Judaism than this claim! Yet this claim lies at the center of the Jesus story. If first-century Palestinian Jews were naturally going to produce a legend, it seems clear that it would not have looked anything like this one. But there are other surprising, radically countercultural aspects to the Jesus story as well. For example:

1. Jews were generally expecting a messiah who would be an inspiring human leader and would liberate them from Roman rule. Instead of this militant, political messiah, however, the Jesus story centers on a God-man who allows himself to be crucified by the very enemies he is supposed to overthrow! If it is not rooted in history, what explains this surprising—even oxymoronic by first-century Jewish standards—new story about the messiah?

2. Jews were generally expecting a messiah who would reinforce the religious establishment and keep the Jewish traditions blamelessly. Yet Jesus's main *opponents* were from among the religious establishment, for he did not meticulously honor Jewish traditions. According to the Gospels, Jesus's entourage consisted of far more sinners, prostitutes, and tax collectors than it did people in good standing with the religious establishment. We might also note the unprecedented honor Jesus showed to women—including women of ill-repute—throughout his ministry. If they are not rooted in his-

tory, what explains these unusual, countercultural aspects of the Jesus story?

3. As N. T. Wright has shown, while many Jews looked forward to a general resurrection of the dead at the end of time, no one in the first century was expecting an *individual* to rise from the dead in the midst of the "present evil age."[24] If it is not rooted in history, what explains this completely new concept that lies at the center of the Jesus story?

4. Whereas myths and legends tend to turn their founders into heroes, the Gospels consistently present the disciples as very average, if not at times exceptionally dull. This remarkably realistic, self-deprecating feature of the Gospel narratives is, we suggest, further evidence of their historicity.

The Explanation of the Earliest Disciples

Legends do not generally arise in contradiction to fundamental convictions held by the culture of those who create and embrace them. Yet if the Jesus story is largely a fictitious legend, this is exactly what we must suppose happened. We submit that the initial historical implausibility of this supposition should be enough for us seriously to consider alternative explanations.

One such explanation is the one given us by those who first told the Jesus story. It is simple and straightforward, and it explains all that needs to be explained—though it requires that we accept the reality of the supernatural. In essence, the earliest disciples tell us that they report what they do about Jesus (despite its conflict with their own cultural/religious expectations) because *this is how things actually happened*. Most importantly, they tell us they believe Jesus is the Son of God and worship him as Lord because, though it violates some of their most fundamental Jewish religious convictions to do so, his life, teachings, miracles, and resurrection convinced them. According to Luke, this is in essence what Peter proclaimed in the first Christian sermon when he preached, "Jesus of Nazareth [was] a man attested to you by God with deeds of power, wonders, and signs that God did through him among you, as you yourselves know. . . . God raised him up, having freed him from death, . . . and of that all of us are witnesses" (Acts 2:22, 24, 32).

This line of conviction is what we find throughout the New Testament. The faith of the earliest disciples was based on God's attestation through "deeds of power, wonders, and signs that God did through him." If this depiction of the earliest disciples is rooted in history, we can begin to understand how some of their most basic religious and cultural assumptions were overturned, how they came to worship Jesus as the embodiment of Yahweh, why their story is full of countercultural elements, and why they were willing to stake their lives on these claims. However, if this depiction is not rooted in history, we are left with questions as to how and why a legend such as this ever arose within the religious environment of first-century Palestinian Judaism.

3

"Long, Long Ago and Far, Far Away?"

The Question of Paul and the Historical Jesus

M yths and legends are generally told about events that occurred in the relatively distant past—"once upon a time; long, long ago; and far, far away." Remarkably enough, the Jesus story is not at all like that. It is located squarely in recent history ("recent" from the perspective of the people telling the story). The Gospels tell us Jesus was born when Augustus was emperor, Quirinius was governor of Syria, and Herod was king of Judea. And Jesus was crucified when Caiaphas was high priest and Pilate was governor. These are very public figures who were household names among Palestinian Jews in the early to mid-first century, not long before the Gospels were written.

Historical markers such as these make explaining the Gospels' portrait of Jesus as merely legend difficult. If it's hard to account for how a legend about a God-man could arise among Jews in first-century Palestine in the first place, it is much harder to explain how it arose as *quickly* as the Jesus story allegedly arose—and in the same geographical region as the events it claims to report. Whatever else we say about the Jesus story, therefore, it seems it was not a story about someone who lived "long, long ago and far, far away." To the original hearers it was, rather, a story about a person who lived very recently and in a nearby region.

The Witness of Paul

The problem of explaining away the Jesus story as largely legendary is exacerbated further when we consider that the Gospels aren't even the earliest Christian writings we possess.[1] Rather, the earliest record of what followers of Jesus believed comes from the apostle Paul. While most scholars date the four Gospels between AD 70 and 100 (see chapter 7), Paul's letters were written between the early 50s and early 60s.[2] What we find in these writings is truly remarkable.

From Paul we learn that the earliest Christians—most of whom were at this time Jews like Paul himself—worshipped Jesus as "Lord" (e.g., Phil. 2:9–11). For first-century Jews, this title was equivalent to "Yahweh" when used in religious contexts. In Paul's letters we also discover that the earliest Christians prayed to Jesus as God (see, e.g., 1 Cor. 1:2; 2 Cor. 12:8–10), referred to Jesus as God (Rom. 9:5; Titus 2:13), and ascribed to Jesus many attributes and activities of God.[3] These earliest Christians also believed that Jesus was crucified for their sins and was then resurrected from the dead (e.g., 1 Cor. 15:3–8). All this was believed about a man who had lived and died just two decades earlier.

What's also clear from Paul's writings, however, is that the earliest Christians didn't *start* believing these things about Jesus two decades after Jesus lived. To the contrary, most scholars agree that a significant amount of the material Paul is passing on to his congregations, including his material on the resurrection and much of the material that most strongly affirms Christ's deity, has a creedal form to it. That is, it is traditional material that had already become somewhat formalized by the time Paul refers to it. This means that this material must have been circulated among the Christian communities a good while before Paul received it and passed it on. Thus, the two-decade window shrinks considerably. In the end, there appears to be very little time for the fictitious development required by the legendary-Jesus thesis. In the words of Richard Bauckham, "The earliest Christology was already the highest Christology."[4]

How are we to explain this? Almost immediately after Jesus lived, we find multitudes of Jews (and later Gentiles) coming to accept—against some of their religious culture's most fundamental presuppositions—that a human being is Lord, God, Creator, and Savior of the world. New Testament authors give us their own explanation for how this most unexpected faith came about. Jesus's extraordinary life and miracles and especially their experience of him after his death convinced them of this interpretation. He was a man "attested to you by God . . . with deeds of power, wonders and signs" (Acts 2:22). If they are telling us the truth, the puzzle is solved. But if we are unwilling to accept their explanation, what plausible alternative is available?

Paul and the Cosmic Savior

Appreciating the difficulty this poses for the legendary-Jesus theory, some legendary-Jesus theorists have proposed a radical solution. What if Paul didn't believe that Jesus was a recent historical figure after all? In this view, Paul had a religious experience of some sort that he identified, for whatever reasons, as an encounter with Jesus (1 Cor. 15:8). But the Jesus he came to believe in and preach was a cosmic redeemer figure in the spirit world, *not a recent contemporary in history*. His view of Jesus was thus something along the lines of the savior deities we know ancient mystery religions embraced: a being who lived and redeemed the world "once upon a time, long, long ago and far, far away."

What then are we to say about the Gospels, each of which portrays Jesus as living, dying, and rising in recent Palestinian history? These scholars argue that this historicized version of the Jesus story was, in its entirety, an intentional fabrication. In essence, these scholars argue, Mark (who most scholars believe wrote the first Gospel) took Paul's cosmic "once upon a time" savior figure and robed him in a fictitious historical narrative. The other Gospel authors followed suit. They thus made it look like Jesus, the cosmic savior of the world, lived very recently—when Herod was king of Judea, Quirinius was governor of Syria, and so forth.

The argument is clever and removes the difficulty of explaining how a legend of a God-man could arise so quickly among first-century Jews. Not only this, but these scholars argue that a close reading of

Paul's writings supports their position. They argue that Paul's letters are devoid of any historical specifics about Jesus. G. A. Wells, for example, argues,

> [Paul's] letters have no allusion to the parents of Jesus, let alone to the virgin birth. They never refer to a place of birth. . . . They give no indication of the time or place of his earthly existence. They do not refer to his trial before a Roman official, nor to Jerusalem as the place of execution. They mention neither John the Baptist, nor Judas, nor Peter's denial of his master. . . . These letters also fail to mention any miracles Jesus is supposed to have worked, a particularly striking omission, since, according to the gospels he worked so many.[5]

On this basis, these adherents of the Christ myth theory argue that the only Jesus Paul knew of was "a divine presence in Christian communities, bestowing revelation and guidance, a channel to God and to knowledge of spiritual truths."[6] In other words, these considerations suggest that the Jesus of Paul and the earliest Christians was little different from the various deities worshiped and experienced within other ancient pagan mystery religions.

The argument is clever, but does it hold water? In what follows, we shall argue that there are problems with the view that the Gospels are historicized fictions, problems with the position that Paul saw Jesus as a nonhistorical, mythical savior who lived and redeemed the world in the distant or cosmic past, and even problems with the claim that Paul's writings lack any historical specifics about Jesus's life.

Could the Gospels Be Historicized Fiction?

There are at least seven major problems with the contention that the Gospels can be understood as historicized fiction:

1. To begin, as we will show in chapter 6, the Gospels simply do not read like a fictional genre of literature. To the contrary, they give us many indications that they genuinely intend to report reliable history. What is more, as we'll see in part 2 of this work, they pass

all the standard tests scholars usually apply to ancient documents
to ascertain a general historical reliability.

2. We have to wonder *why* the authors of the Gospels would want to
   create a new, fictionalized Jesus story. What was their motivation?
   Remember that by the time these authors were writing their accounts, Christians around the Roman Empire were being tortured
   and put to death for their faith. (Nero launched the first Roman
   persecution in AD 64.) So what could these authors have thought
   they or their readers would gain by fabricating and embracing this
   fictional story?

3. Regardless of why one imagines the Gospel authors would write
   these fictional accounts, we have to wonder why any early Christian
   would have accepted them as true. We're being asked to accept that
   for decades early Christians believed in a Jesus who lived "long,
   long ago and far, far away," and then, quite suddenly, Mark and the
   other Gospel authors presented a new Jesus who purportedly lived
   in the very recent past. Why would these early Christians, who had
   much to lose by being wrong, accept such a notion?

4. We have to wonder how these authors thought they could have
   gotten away with creating a fiction situated in the recent past and
   in such close geographical proximity to their audiences. We must
   remember that Jewish religious authorities had a vested interest in
   putting an end to this movement, which they considered to be a
   dangerous sect. If the story these authors were telling was false, it
   seems it would have been relatively easy to expose it as such.

   Consider that, even with a most liberal dating of the Gospels
   (approximately AD 70 to 100, see chapter 7), some of the Gospel
   authors' contemporaries would have been alive at the time when
   they were allegedly fabricating their historicized fictions. Not only
   this, but as we have said, these authors wove their story around a
   number of well-known public figures—people like Caiaphas, Herod,
   and Pilate. Would not such name dropping have made their story
   extremely vulnerable to falsification? Interestingly enough, however,
   while Jewish and Gentile opponents of Christianity offer many
   arguments against this new religion, no one in ancient history ever
   accused Christians of making the whole thing up. Indeed, no one in

the ancient world disputed that Jesus existed or that he performed extraordinary feats (more on this in chapter 10).

5. To accept the version of early church history offered by these legendary-Jesus theorists, we must also accept that the version of church history given in the book of Acts is largely false. While it would take us too far astray to discuss this matter in this work, there are many reasons to conclude that the book of Acts is a remarkably reliable piece of ancient historiography.[7] All of these considerations are also reasons for rejecting this and every other version of the legendary-Jesus thesis.

6. This understanding of the Gospels as fiction completely ignores the role that writing plays in orally dominant cultures. As we'll see throughout part 2 of this work, it is of paramount importance that we remember that writing was not the primary means of communication among people in the first century. Rather, information was passed along primarily by word of mouth. This is what we mean when we refer to it as an "orally dominant"—or "orally oriented"—culture (which is significantly different from an exclusively oral culture in which writing does not yet exist).

A host of studies done over the last several decades on orally dominant cultures has demonstrated that writing plays a very different role in these cultures than it does in "literary cultures"—cultures in which writing is a primary means of communication. In literary cultures such as our own, novelty and innovation in literature is valued. In orally dominant cultures, however, it is generally frowned upon. The primary purpose of writing, rather, is faithfully to re-express—or activate—an established oral tradition.[8]

In this light, the idea that the Gospel authors would have been inclined to come up with a new, fictional story of Jesus must be judged as seriously suspect. Among other things, it is a largely anachronistic notion. It imagines the Gospel authors as something like modern authors of fiction, writing within a literary, rather than an orally oriented, culture.

7. Finally, and closely related to this, recent orality studies have suggested that oral traditions—particularly relatively recent, religiously oriented traditions—in orally dominant contexts tend to be quite resistant to change in terms of the essential components. As we

will discuss in more detail in chapter 5, oral performers (or "tradents")—those who regularly recite oral traditions for their communities—are allowed a certain amount of flexibility in how they recite traditional material. But if the oral performer alters anything of substance in the tradition, members of the community customarily interrupt and correct him or her.[9] Hence, the suggestion that a fictional writing from an anonymous author could have overturned established oral traditions about Jesus in the early church must be judged as massively improbable. This is simply not how orally dominant cultures tend to operate.

Paul and the Recently Resurrected Jesus

There are also serious problems with the contention that Paul viewed Jesus along the lines of the savior deities found in ancient mystery religions—beings who lived and redeemed the world "long, long ago and far, far away."

1. The very suggestion that a first-century Jew like Paul would have been open to being influenced by religious ideas found in ancient mystery religions is problematic. As we saw in chapter 2, Jews were, on the whole, resistant to pagan religious ideas. Their religious tradition was rooted in historical events and ran directly counter to the sort of "once upon a time in a supermundane region" mythical thinking that characterized mystery religions. If Paul knew about any of the "once upon a time" savior figures found in ancient mystery religions, we have every reason to assume he would have viewed them as just another example of heathen depravity.

For this reason, we must conclude that the notion that Paul, a former Pharisee, propagated a new religion modeled after these pagan religions is highly improbable. But the improbability is increased even further when we consider that we don't have any clear evidence that mystery religions even existed until the late second or early third century. Drawing conclusions about the religious environment of first-century Palestine on the basis of evidence from other locations that date one to two hundred years later is anachronistic, to say the least. It is rooted in baseless speculation, not historical evidence.

2. The argument that Paul believed in a Jesus who lived "long, long ago and far, far away" conflicts with the fact that Paul refers to James, who was still alive at the time of Paul's writing, as "the Lord's brother" (Gal. 1:19). Clearly, if Paul knew the brother of Jesus was still alive when he was writing, he must have believed Jesus was a very recent contemporary.

Those who insist Paul viewed Jesus as a cosmic redeemer figure in the distant past attempt to argue that the phrase "the Lord's brother" refers not to Jesus's *biological* brother but to "a small group or fraternity of Messianists . . . zealous in the service of the risen one."[10] There were a number of subgroups within the early church with different designations, they argue, and one of them was known as "the brothers of the Lord." The response is far from compelling, however.

It is true that, at least at Corinth, there were subgroups within the early church who aligned themselves with certain people—e.g., Paul, Apollos, Cephas, and Christ (1 Cor. 1:11–13). But there's no evidence any group was called "the brothers of the Lord." Not only this, but it is important to realize that Paul *chastised* the immature Corinthians for having such cliques. We have every reason to conclude, therefore, that if there had been a group that identified themselves as "the brothers of the Lord," Paul would not have acknowledged it as a legitimate group by identifying an individual (James) with this designation. There is, then, no reason to interpret "the Lord's brother" in any sense other than biological, which means Paul indeed viewed Jesus to be a recent contemporary.

3. The notion that Paul viewed Jesus as a cosmic savior who lived in the distant past seems to directly contradict Paul's list of those Jesus appeared to in 1 Corinthians 15:3–8. These eyewitnesses were contemporaries of Paul, and most of them, including the apostles, were still alive at the time of Paul's writing (see v. 6). Since Paul obviously believed Jesus appeared to various people in the recent past, it seems very reasonable to conclude he believed Jesus lived, died, and rose in the recent past.

Not so, argue some legendary-Jesus theorists. While Paul believed Jesus *appeared* in the recent past, they argue, he nevertheless viewed him as living, dying, and rising in the distant past. In other words, these scholars postulate an indefinitely long period of time between Jesus's life, death, burial, and resurrection, on the one hand, and his appearance to the eyewitnesses Paul lists, on the other. We do not see that this suggestion has any merit to it—other than the fact that it helps relieve legendary-

Jesus theorists of the burden of explaining how a fictional legend about a contemporary Jew being the embodiment of Yahweh could have arisen so quickly within first-century Jewish culture.

The fact that Paul lists James, the Lord's brother, as one to whom Jesus appeared is enough to refute the suggestion. But even beyond this, inserting an indefinite period of time between Jesus's life, death, and resurrection, on the one hand, and his appearance to the people Paul lists in 1 Corinthians, on the other, is completely unnatural to the text. Paul simply states that Jesus "died for our sins, . . . that he was buried, and that he was raised on the third day, . . . and that he appeared to Cephas, then to the twelve," and others (vv. 3–5). The passage gives the clear impression that Paul is describing a closely connected nexus of events. Inserting a virtual epoch between "raised on the third day" and "he appeared" strikes us as a desperate ad hoc hypothesis created for the sole purpose of salvaging the theory that Paul viewed Jesus as a figure who lived "long, long ago and far, far away."

4. Finally, in 1 Thessalonians 2:14–16 Paul identifies the Jews who "killed the Lord Jesus" as the same ones who were presently hindering Paul and his colleagues from preaching the gospel. This suggests that Paul believed Jesus lived, died, and was resurrected in the recent past.

Those legendary-Jesus theorists who argue that Paul believed Jesus lived in the distant past attempt to get around this difficulty by insisting that these three verses were inserted into this letter by a later editor. But there is simply no compelling evidence for this conclusion. All extant ancient copies of 1 Thessalonians contain these verses. Some try to make their case by arguing that the syntax, vocabulary, and even the theology of this passage is not characteristic of Paul, but none of these arguments are particularly compelling, as we have argued elsewhere.[11]

The Lack of Historical Specifics about Jesus's Life

We've seen there are problems with the contention that the Gospels are historicized fictions as well as with the contention that Paul believed Jesus lived in the distant past. But what are we to make of the claim that Paul's letters lack any reference to details about Jesus's life? Two broad points may be made.

First, it's important to remember that all Paul's letters were written in response to particular problems with which individual congregations were struggling. We thus shouldn't expect to find instruction on the details of Jesus's life and teachings unless doing so would have helped solve one of those specific issues for a congregation. In this light, it shouldn't surprise us if Paul didn't have much occasion in any of his extant writings to review many of the details of Jesus's life such as we find in the Gospels.

At the same time, there are good reasons to suppose that Paul and his congregations knew at least the basic facts of Jesus's life. Indeed, once we accept that Paul's message was centered on a man who lived just a few decades earlier, it's extremely difficult to imagine how he could have made his message compelling to people without such information. How could his potential converts not have wanted to know about the person they were being asked to surrender their lives to and put their lives at risk for?

This point takes on even more force when we realize that Paul held up Jesus's life as *the model* for everyone to imitate (1 Cor. 11:1; 2 Cor. 8:9; 10:1; Rom. 15:2–3; Eph. 5:1; Phil. 2:5–7; 3:8–10). How could Paul and others possibly aspire to be like Jesus, to be "conformed to his image" (Rom. 8:29), unless they had significant biographical information about him?

Second, evidence that Paul knew significant details about the historical Jesus is found in the fact that some of this information creeps through in his epistles. For example, Paul knew that Jesus was born and raised as a Jew (Gal. 4:4) and that he was a descendant of Abraham and David (Gal. 3:16; Rom. 1:3). He knew that Jesus had a brother named James (Gal. 1:19), as we've seen, and perhaps other unnamed brothers as well (1 Cor. 9:5). He knew by name a number of disciples who ministered with Jesus, and he knew that the disciple Peter was married (1 Cor. 9:5; 15:3–7).

Paul also knew that Jesus was betrayed (1 Cor. 11:23) and that he was executed by crucifixion (1 Cor. 1:17–18; Gal. 5:11; 6:12; Phil. 2:8; 3:18) with the help of certain contemporary Judean Jews (1 Thess. 2:14–15). He was aware of the fact that Jesus instituted a memorial meal the night before his death (1 Cor. 11:23–25) and that Jesus was buried after his death and was resurrected three days later (Rom. 4:24–25; cf. Rom. 6:4–9; 8:11, 34; 1 Cor. 6:14; 2 Cor. 4:14; Gal. 1:1; 1 Thess. 4:14). Indeed, as we have seen, he was aware that a number of contemporary people were eyewitnesses of the risen Christ (1 Cor. 15:4–8). Not only this, but Paul's writings contain many phrases that suggest he was aware of various orally circulated versions of some of Jesus's teachings.[12]

Perhaps even more importantly for our purposes, Paul knew that Jesus's earthly life was characterized by meekness, gentleness, self-sacrificial love, and humble service (2 Cor. 10:1; Phil. 2:5–7). As we already mentioned, Paul's central passion was to know and be conformed to Jesus Christ (Phil. 3:8–10), and it's no coincidence that Paul's own thought, attitude, and conduct paralleled closely what we find in the Jesus of the Gospels. Nor can it be considered a coincidence that Paul's healing ministry, his welcoming of sinners, and his life of poverty and humble service closely paralleled Jesus's life and ministry as recorded in the Gospels. Paul practiced what he preached, and at the foundation of what he preached was a body of knowledge about the ministry and character of the Lord he served.

We thus conclude that not only did Paul and all early Christians believe Jesus was a recent contemporary, but they also knew a good bit of information about him—enough to model their lives after him.

Conclusion

All of this confronts us once again with the question, How are we to explain first-century Jews like Paul, Peter, and John coming to place their faith in and worship a contemporary Jewish man as the embodiment of Yahweh? Indeed, how are we to explain how a Jewish man (James) came to have faith in and worship *his own brother* as the embodiment of Yahweh? The legendary hypothesis seems to be blocked at every turn. We don't have the right culture and certainly don't have enough time for a legend of this magnitude to arise.

If the historical Jesus was close to how Paul and the Gospels present him, we can begin to understand how the earliest Jewish disciples, including Jesus's own brother, came to believe in him, against some of their most fundamental religious and cultural convictions. And we can begin to understand why they were willing to lay their lives on the line for the truthfulness of their radically countercultural faith. If the historical Jesus was not like Paul and the Gospels present him, however—worse, if he never existed—we are left only with unanswerable questions. However difficult it may be to accept that the Gospels' portrait of Jesus is rooted in history, we submit that accepting it as substantially legendary is even more so.

4

Rising Gods, Legendary Heroes, and Divinized Teachers

How Unique Is the Jesus Story?

T hus far we have argued there is no warrant for people to foreclose the possibility that miraculous events on occasion occur. While we are justi-fied in preferring naturalistic explanations over ones that appeal to super-natural influences, all things being equal, we are not justified in insisting on naturalistic explanations regardless of how much the evidence points in a different direction. We've also argued that first-century Palestinian Judaism was a most unlikely environment for a legend about a miracle-working God-man to arise, let alone arise virtually overnight—that is, while the brother, mother, and close friends of the man who was being divinized were still alive. Considerations like this show the legendary-Jesus thesis to be implausible and thus force us to seriously consider the possibility that the story early Christians told about Jesus was rooted in history.

Still, there are other reasons people give for interpreting the Jesus story as predominantly legendary in nature. I (Greg) first came across the objection we will consider in this chapter as a university freshman. I had become a Christian about a year earlier, but my faith was already starting to weaken. Among other things, I had a smart, persistent, agnostic father who constantly raised questions I couldn't answer. But nothing rocked my faith like my first class in biblical literature at the University of Minnesota. There I learned that stories of dying and rising gods, virgin births, and miracle workers were widespread when the Gospels were written. Here I had been basing my life for the last year on the mistaken conviction that Jesus was something unique! Within a short time, I abandoned my belief in Jesus, in the Bible, in God, and in just about everything. (I obviously came back to it at a later date—but we will leave that for chapter 12.)

Simply put, a common argument put forward by legendary-Jesus theorists goes as follows: The Jesus story shares many similarities with other myths and fictitious legends; therefore, it too should be considered a myth or fictitious legend.[1] These supposed similarities, or "parallels," roughly fall into three categories.

First, as mentioned above, we know of tales of dying and rising gods in the ancient world. Some argue that the Jesus story is simply a variation of this genre of mythic tale.[2] Second, history is full of stories of mythical and legendary heroes who, like Jesus, were said to be born to a virgin, had their life threatened while infants, were called a son of a god, and so forth. Some contend that the Jesus of the Gospels is simply another example of these mythic heroes.[3] And finally, we occasionally find in history individuals who were said to have performed miracles and who were sometimes even worshipped as divine in their own lifetime or shortly thereafter. Some argue that we can understand the birth of Christianity, with its unusual claims and surprising attitude about Jesus, as just another example of this peculiar religious phenomenon.

At first glance (for example, as a university freshman!) it may appear the argument against the historicity of the Jesus story on the basis of parallels is quite strong. When examined more closely, however, we maintain that it does not carry much weight.

Dying and Rising Gods

At least four considerations lead us to the conclusion that these supposed "dying and rising god" myths bear little relationship to the Jesus story or that these alleged parallels in any way call into question the historicity of the Jesus story.

1. To begin, the very category of ancient "dying and rising gods" has been called into question by most contemporary scholars. In short, when each of these myths is analyzed in detail, it turns out that either there is no actual death, no actual resurrection, or no actual "god" in the first place! As J. Z. Smith notes, "The category of dying and rising gods, once a major topic of scholarly investigation, must now be understood to have been largely a misnomer based on imaginative reconstructions and exceedingly late or highly ambiguous texts."[4]

2. Even if we grant that certain pagan myths parallel the story of Jesus's resurrection in some respects, this doesn't itself mean that the story of Jesus's resurrection is not historical. Indeed, as we shall argue in chapter 12, if it's true that God is a God who loves, who became a human, and who died for our salvation, and if it's true that we are made in his image, then we should *expect* that an intuition pointing in this direction, expressed through legend and myth, would be found among people at different times and places.

3. The presence of pagan parallels might negatively affect our estimation of the historicity of the Jesus story *if* it could be demonstrated that there was a line of historical influence flowing from one or more of the pagan myths to the early followers of Jesus. The vast majority of scholars agree that this is entirely implausible, however, and for good reason.

For one thing, there is simply no evidence for a line of influence from pagan stories to the early Christians. Indeed, with the exception of Osiris, all the written accounts of these myths date *after* the birth of Christianity. Moreover, as we argued in chapter 2, we have no reason to suppose that monotheistic Galilean Jews in the first century would have found anything attractive about these sorts of pagan stories. To the contrary, the evidence suggests that their revulsion toward these sorts of stories made them more, not less, staunch in their monotheistic Judaism.

4. Scholars agree that ancient myths surrounding the ostensive death and resuscitation of a god were associated with seasonal vegetation cycles. They express the wonder of the death-rebirth cycle of fall and winter by telling of things that happened "once upon a time" in the mythic past. The Jesus story, however, could hardly be more different from this. Jesus's birth, ministry, death, and resurrection are located not in a "once upon

a time" mythic past but in recent history—i.e., when Augustus was emperor of Rome, Quirinius was governor of Syria, Pilate was governor of Palestine, Herod was king of the Jews, and Joseph of Arimathea was a member of the Sanhedrin (see, e.g., Matt. 2:1; 27:2; Mark 15:1; 15:43; Luke 2:1–2; John 19:38.) There is no precedent for telling a story of a supposedly dying and rising god *in identifiable history*, let alone in *recent* identifiable history, let alone in a *Jewish environment* that was intrinsically hostile to such stories.

More specifically, when one examines the details of the various mythic accounts of dying and rising gods, the difference between them and the Jesus story becomes even more pronounced. According to one version of the Osiris story, for example, Osiris was killed by his brother, chopped up into fourteen pieces, and scattered throughout Egypt. Isis then rescued all but one of his body parts, reassembled them, and brought him back to life. He was then given rulership of the underworld. To claim that this account parallels the Jesus story is, in our opinion, quite a stretch. Indeed, it's not even clear we should call it a *resurrection* account since Osiris was never fully reconstituted. Not only this, but poor Osiris really wasn't brought back to "life" at all, since his resuscitated rulership remained *in the realm of the dead*!

We grant that one can discern in this and other "dying and rising god" myths a vague intuition that death must be defeated by a god. In this limited sense there is an echo of the proclamation we find in the culmination of the Jesus story (we'll say more about this in chapter 12). But beyond this, there is nothing that the pagan stories and the Jesus story have in common, and thus there is no reason to suspect that the Jesus story is influenced by, or bears any significant relationship to, the pagan stories.

Jesus as a Mythic Hero

It cannot be denied that the Jesus of the Gospels fits many of the classic features of mythic heroes. But we don't see that this in any way undermines the claim that the Jesus story is substantially rooted in history. We offer four considerations.

1. Even if we grant that Jesus is a classic "mythic hero," this does not necessarily mean that he is not *also* a historical figure. As various

scholars have shown, Abraham Lincoln, John F. Kennedy, and William ("Braveheart") Wallace all fit the classic mythic hero pattern as well, but no one judges them to be nonhistorical for that reason. As Charles Murgia points out, "Conformity [to a mythic pattern] does not necessarily mean that the events did not occur."[5]

2. As we argued above with regard to dying and rising gods, if the portrait of Jesus in the Gospels is grounded in history, we should expect mythic stories to echo it. Think of this along the lines of the people who had encountered aliens in Spielberg's classic movie *Close Encounters of the Third Kind*. Once "touched," these people couldn't resist compulsively sculpting or drawing a certain plateau—though they had no idea why. It turns out their compulsion was a sort of homing device placed in them to lead them to the Devil's Tower in Wyoming. There the aliens were going to have a rendezvous with humanity, and these people were invited. Some who had the "homing device" discovered the reality to which it pointed, but most did not. They just sculpted and drew mythological echoes of the real thing, as it were.

Similarly, we may interpret various hero myths (as well as the stories of dying and rising gods discussed above) as expressions of an inner homing device. We've been touched by "the light of the world" who wants to rendezvous with us in the person of Jesus Christ. People express in mythic form truths that in various ways seem to echo the Jesus story because Jesus *is* the light of the world who shines in every heart, to the extent a person's heart is open to him (cf. John 1:6–10).

3. While Jesus fits most of the traits of a mythic hero, the Jesus story also lacks some of the most standard features of hero myths. For example, the Gospels depict Jesus as a teacher, healer, and exorcist, but these are not classic traits of mythic heroes. Conversely, Jesus is not depicted as an earthly heroic warrior or king, which most mythic heroes are. These differences suggest that, while the Jesus story certainly addresses the hope typically expressed in hero myths, the story itself is not simply a hero myth.

4. Finally, the only way one can reliably determine the extent to which any ancient account is historical is by examining historical evidence, not by attempting to find parallels in mythic stories. The reason scholars accept that, for example, Lincoln, Kennedy, and Wallace were historic while Hercules, Achilles, and Asclepios were not—despite the fact that

both groups have many stereotypical heroic myth traits—is because of historical evidence. So too, in order to determine whether the Jesus story is rooted in history or is a myth or legend, we have to examine historical evidence. We submit that when this is done fairly, it becomes exceedingly difficult to deny that the story is solidly rooted in history.

Legend-Making Parallels to the Jesus Movement

What should we make of the fact that at certain times in history figures seem to have inspired supernatural stories about themselves and evoked worship during their own lifetime or shortly thereafter? Does the existence of this occasional phenomenon undermine the uniqueness of the early Jesus movement? To answer this question we would need to examine each alleged parallel on a case-by-case basis. In what follows we will examine the three cases that seem strongly to parallel the early Jesus movement and that are frequently cited in support of the legendary-Jesus perspective.

Apollonius of Tyana

One of the legends most frequently appealed to by legendary-Jesus theorists as a parallel to Jesus concerns a second-century itinerant teacher and wonder-worker named Apollonius of Tyana. It is reported that he healed people, raised the dead, predicted the future, exorcized demons, and appeared to some of his followers after his death. He was later worshipped as a god by devotees who formed a religious cult that was centered on him.[6] Some have argued that it's inconsistent for Christians to reject the historicity of reports of Apollonius's supernatural feats while accepting the historicity of the Gospels' reports about Jesus's supernatural feats. If one assumes the stories of Apollonius are legendary, one ought to assume the same for the stories about Jesus. We find this line of reasoning to be questionable for the following reasons:

1. The first thing that needs to be said in response to this argument is that there's no reason to assume that the reports of Apollonius's extraordinary feats are entirely legendary. We agree that one can't

simply pick and choose on the basis of personal preference which reports of the supernatural one is going to accept. One has to fairly assess the evidence on a case-by-case basis. As a matter of fact, while the evidence regarding Apollonius's life is much more scanty and questionable than what we have with regard to Jesus, as we shall see, it nevertheless strikes us as sufficient to warrant the conclusion that there probably was a man named Apollonius who somehow performed some rather impressive feats, especially in the areas of healing people and of casting out demons.

At the same time, however, we have to appreciate the significant differences that exist between the account of Apollonius and the Gospels' account of Jesus. The Jesus story, we argue, is on much firmer ground historically speaking than the account of Apollonius. The remaining points address this issue.

2. The sheer fact that the stories of Apollonius's wonder-working feats arose in a pagan environment that was conducive to the creation of legends about miracle-working divine men sets them in a different context than the stories about Jesus. While we deem it more likely than not that some of the stories about Apollonius are rooted in historical events, it is also easier to explain how stories about Apollonius were expanded in this legendary direction than it is in the case of Jesus.

3. The only account we have of Apollonius's life was written more than a century after Apollonius lived, giving ample time in this environment for stories about his life to expand. In the case of Jesus, however, we have five sources (the four Gospels and Paul) written within several decades of his life. Not only this, but as we shall see in chapter 5, each of these accounts give us indications they are passing on reliable oral material that predates them.

4. Apollonius's biographer (Philostratus) was paid by a wealthy empress to compose a positive account of Apollonius, giving him a motive to make Apollonius look good. Those who preached and wrote about Jesus do not seem to have had these sorts of financial or political motives. To the contrary, given their cultural situation, they would have to have known that proclaiming their radically countercultural message to the world would likely cost them a great deal—which it did.

5. Christianity had been around for almost two centuries when Philostratus wrote his account of Apollonius, and it may very well have been that certain aspects of the Jesus story were incorporated into the Apollonius story for competitive-evangelistic purposes.

6. Philostratus, to his credit, acknowledges that he is relying on another written source as well as on hearsay, and his account is appropriately filled with tentative language (e.g., "it is reported that . . ."). The Gospels, by contrast, claim to be passing on information that is rooted in eyewitness testimony, and they read like they are grounded in just such an eyewitness perspective.[7]

7. Finally, there is nothing within Philostratus's account that buttresses our confidence in the historical reliability of his material. Indeed, his account contains several blatant historical errors. Nor is his material supported by external evidence, such as confirmation in other available written sources or from archaeology. By contrast, as we shall see in chapters 7–11, the Gospels give us many reasons to conclude that they are generally reliable.

In light of this, while it seems more probable than not that a man named Apollonius lived and somehow performed certain extraordinary feats, it is much easier to explain how stories about him expanded in a legendary direction over time than it is in the case of Jesus.

Sabbatai Sevi

A second alleged parallel to Jesus concerns an unusual seventeenth-century Jewish messianic figure named Sabbatai Sevi. In and around the time Sevi lived, he was hailed by his followers as the messiah, is reported to have performed miracles, and was even said by some to have risen from the dead.[8] If we judge these claims about Sevi to be legendary, despite the fact that some of the claims arose in Sevi's own lifetime, why can we not judge the claims about Jesus to be legendary, even if some arose in Jesus's own lifetime? The fact that those who followed Sevi were Jews, not pagans, just as was the case with Jesus, arguably strengthens the parallel.

On the surface the parallel looks quite impressive. But when we examine it more closely, much of it falls apart. We offer four considerations:

1. The reports of Sabbatai's miracles are very conflicting. Most significantly, his closest confidant, the "prophet Nathan" stated that
   Sabbatai's messiahship involved a test to see whether the Jews would
   "believe without any sign or miracle."[9] Unlike the case with Apollonius, therefore, we find no compelling reason to suppose there is any
   historical evidence behind the stories of Sevi's miracles. By contrast,
   not only did none of Jesus's followers deny that Jesus did miracles,
   but there's no record of *anyone* in the ancient world—including his
   enemies—denying that Jesus did miracles (see chapter 10).

2. The several conflicting accounts of Sevi's "occultation" (supernatural
   liberation from death to the heavenly world) that circulated after his
   death can be shown to have gone through several stages of legendary
   development and are, in any case, obviously legendary in nature.
   For example, in one account a dragon is said to have guarded Sevi's
   tomb. This strongly contrasts with the accounts of Jesus's resurrection found in the four Gospels and in Paul's epistles. While there
   are differences between these five accounts (they obviously weren't
   copied verbatim from one another), they are reasonably consistent
   (see chapter 9). Moreover, they are not characterized by the sort
   of fantasy that is typically associated with fictionally embellished
   legends.

3. No one claimed to have seen Sevi after he allegedly rose from the
   dead. (This obviously raises questions about how anyone was supposed to know Sevi rose, but legends often leave questions like
   this unanswered.) By contrast, the Gospels and Paul's epistles list
   numerous eyewitnesses to the resurrected Jesus.

4. It is not difficult to explain the stories of Sevi's miracles and resurrection as legends that served a sociological purpose. The stories
   were in keeping with the cultural beliefs, attitudes, and apocalyptic
   expectations of the people who told them. More specifically, the
   Jews who told these stories about Sevi were well acquainted with,
   and lived in tension with, Christianity. It's thus not difficult to explain them as polemical counters to Christian claims about Jesus.
   By contrast, as we've said, the Jesus story runs directly counter to
   some of the most fundamental aspects of the culture in which the
   story is being told. For example, the claim itself arose from within
   a cultural context in which there was no conceptual space for the

idea of an *individual* resurrection prior to the dawning of the messianic "age to come."

In light of all this, we conclude that, while the movement surrounding Sabbatai Sevi is certainly curious and speaks to the atypical speed with which legends can arise when accompanied by favorable circumstances, it does not parallel the early Jesus movement in any significant way. We need not postulate that Sevi actually performed miracles or rose from the dead to explain why certain people claimed he performed miracles and rose from the dead. In this case, a legendary explanation suffices. In the case of Jesus, we maintain, it simply does not.

Simon Kimbangu

A third and, in our opinion, most impressive alleged parallel to the early Jesus movement concerns a twentieth-century miracle worker in the Congo named Simon Kimbangu. A number of eyewitnesses report that he performed many miracles and exorcisms and even apparently raised several people from the dead. As a result, some of his followers worshiped him as God (not just *a* god, as with Apollonius).[10] What are we to make of this? Does it support the case for viewing the Jesus story as substantially legendary? On the contrary we believe the case of Kimbangu actually supports the case for viewing the Jesus story as substantially rooted in history. Consider three closely related observations:

1. Unlike Apollonius and Sevi (and other alleged parallel figures), in the case of Kimbangu we believe we have to grant that we are dealing with a phenomenon that in significant respects parallels the early Jesus movement. True, the Congo people who worshiped Kimbangu and told stories of his amazing deeds lived within a culture that was quite open to the idea of multiple deities, and in this respect they differ markedly from the monotheistic Jews who first followed Jesus. Still, since there is no obvious motive for the witnesses substantially to distort the truth and no evidence that they did, we see no reason to deny that the reports are essentially historical. No doubt there is exaggeration and embellishment involved, but we find it difficult fully to account for the gist of the reports

without accepting that Kimbangu actually performed a number of the miracles attributed to him.

In this light, we conclude that some of the miracle stories surrounding Kimbangu do not constitute an example of how fast legends can arise. Rather, we find that they provide compelling grounds for concluding that miracles of the sort reported about Jesus *can and do actually occur*. Not only this, but it is important to note that Kimbangu was a Christian minister who performed his miracles "in Jesus's name." So, far from being an argument *against* the truth claims of the earliest followers of Jesus, it rather seems to us that Kimbangu's ministry constitutes further evidence *for* these truth claims.

2. But what about the fact that some of Kimbangu's followers worshipped him as God? Does this perhaps parallel the way in which early Christians worshipped Jesus as God?

   In one respect it obviously does. In both movements people witnessed remarkable feats that led them to embrace a remarkable conclusion: a fellow contemporary human being was God! But there is a significant difference between the religious worldview of people in the twentieth-century Congo and that of the first-century Palestinian Jews.

   The Congo natives Kimbangu ministered to were steeped in an animistic and polytheistic worldview. That is, they believed that divinity resided in various objects and people and that certain humans could channel this inherent divinity in specific directions through magic. As such, these people had little difficulty identifying a man as God in response to the miracles he performed. Indeed, in light of the miracles Kimbangu performed, some obviously found it difficult *not* to confuse him with God.

   By contrast, nothing could be more foreign to the mind of a first-century Palestinian Jew than to identify a fellow human as God. If it's hard to explain how certain animists in the Congo developed a faith in Kimbangu as God without accepting as substantially factual their reports of his miracles, how much harder is it to explain how certain monotheistic Jews embraced Jesus's divinity unless we also accept their reports about his miracles?

3. Closely related to this, there is no evidence Kimbangu ever claimed to be divine or accepted worship directed toward him. (Since he was a Christian minister, we would be surprised if there *was* evidence to this effect.) The movement that claimed Kimbangu was divine and worshipped him as such was polytheistic in nature, and it seems they understandably drew mistaken and overzealous conclusions from the supernatural deeds they witnessed at the hands of a Christian minister. (Compare Paul and Barnabas's similar experience of misunderstanding within the context of the polytheistic culture at Lystra in Acts 14:8–18.) By contrast, there are indications that Jesus *saw himself* as divine and consequently accepted worship. Even apart from the Gospel evidence to this effect, it's difficult to imagine how the practice of worshipping Jesus arose so quickly among his Jewish, monotheistic followers unless it was, in some fashion and to some degree, inspired by him.[11]

Conclusion

We see that, while there are vague commonalities between the Jesus story and ancient stories of gods surviving death, hero myths, and legends surrounding other historical figures, none of these commonalities gives us reason to doubt that the Jesus story is substantially rooted in history. To the contrary, to the extent that these commonalities are legitimate, they are what we should expect if the Jesus story is in fact rooted in history. That is, if God was in fact present in Jesus's birth, ministry, death, and resurrection, as the Gospels say, it's not surprising we find echoes of this story in the myths and legends of people throughout history.

At the same time, however, when examined on a case-by-case basis, most of the alleged parallels break down *in terms of their historical rootedness*. Most importantly, we find nothing in literature or history that significantly parallels the birth of the first-century Jesus movement. Nowhere else do we confront a question as difficult to answer in naturalistic terms as the question we face with respect to this movement. How are we to account for first-century, monotheistic Jews coming to worship a fellow contemporary as the embodiment of Yahweh, while still retaining an obvious commitment to monotheism?

These early followers of Jesus give us their own explanation. They came to faith in Jesus because of the claims he made, the miracles he performed, the extraordinary life he lived, and, most importantly, his resurrection from the dead. If we deny that these claims are rooted in history, what can we postulate as the sufficient explanation for why these disciples came to the faith they did, and what accounts for them giving the explanation they themselves give as to why they believe what they believe? Apart from the basic account of the matter given by the early Christians themselves, there is no clear, historically plausible answer to this question.

5

Oral Traditions and Legend-Making

How Reliable Were the Early Church's
Oral Traditions about Jesus?

As we mentioned in chapter 3, first-century Jewish culture was what scholars today would call an orally dominant culture. While a certain percentage of people could read and write (see below), information was for the most part passed on by word of mouth (and even written texts tended to use "oral-like" techniques of expression). This is why scholars agree that before (and even after) the Gospels were written, early Christians relied primarily, if not exclusively, on oral traditions for their information about Jesus.

For this reason, with regard to assessing the reliability of the Gospels' portrait of Jesus, a good deal hangs on how reliable, or unreliable, one judges the early oral Jesus traditions to be. Those who argue that the Jesus story is largely (or entirely) legendary typically argue that oral transmission is, in general, a very *unreliable* way of passing on information. Hence, however the Jesus story originated—whether it goes back to Jesus or to the spiritual revelations of Paul—these scholars hold that the early Christian view of Jesus evolved rather dramatically over time as it was passed on by word of mouth.[1]

The Classic Form Critical View of the Early Oral Jesus Tradition

The view that the oral traditions of the early Jesus movement were unreliable became a widespread conviction within New Testament scholarship with the advent of a discipline known as "form criticism" in the early twentieth century. This discipline identifies and investigates different literary forms found in the Gospels—parables, sayings, miracle stories, and others. Form criticism then attempts to determine why particular parables, sayings, miracle stories, and such, came into being and evolved the way they did in the social environment of the early church.

A number of considerations led most form critics to conclude that the oral traditions about Jesus in the early church were not historically reliable. For our purposes, we can limit our discussion to four widespread assumptions that played (and continue to play) a particularly important role in the formation of this skeptical stance.

1. It has been widely assumed by form critics that for several decades the early Christian movement was entirely devoid of written texts and, thus, that writing played no regulative role in the transmission of material about Jesus. With no authoritative writing to keep oral traditions in check, it has been widely assumed that oral material about Jesus was easily altered and distorted in the process of transmission.

2. It has been widely assumed by New Testament form critics that oral traditions aren't capable of passing on extended narratives, which is one of the reasons many critical New Testament scholars have assumed that the narrative framework, within which the various literary forms are found in the Gospels, was created by the Gospel authors themselves. That is, the basic narrative of the life of Jesus as offered in the Gospels is not rooted in history.

3. It has been widely assumed that people within orally dominant communities have little genuinely historical interest. That is, it has been assumed that the needs and interests of the community *in the present* shape oral performances much more than a concern to relate past events and teachings accurately. Hence, it has been assumed by form critics that the oral Jesus material arose more out of needs within the community than out of true historical remembrance.

4. Finally, it has been widely assumed by form critics that individuals play little role in the origination, transmission, and regulation of oral traditions. Communities, not individuals, pass on oral traditions. Hence, it's been generally assumed that the eyewitnesses of Jesus (if there were any) would have played little or no regulative role with respect to the direction taken by the early oral traditions about Jesus. Without eyewitness safeguards, the oral traditions about Jesus could be easily altered.

Clearly, if each of these assumptions is correct, the legendary-Jesus thesis becomes more plausible. At the same time, it's important not to exaggerate the significance of our assessment of the pre-Gospel oral Jesus traditions. As we've already seen, our earliest snapshot of what the original followers of Jesus believed comes from Paul, not the Gospels. As we saw in chapter 3, from Paul we learn that within two decades of Jesus's life it was already common for Christians to understand and worship Jesus as the very embodiment of Yahweh. This means there was little to no time for the early Christian view of Jesus to significantly change prior to being inscribed by Paul. So, even apart from the question of the reliability of the oral traditions behind the Gospels, we are strongly confronted with the question of how we can plausibly account for the Jesus story within a first-century, monotheistic, Jewish environment without accepting that it's solidly rooted in history.

Nevertheless, as it concerns the more specific question of the reliability of the Gospels' portrait of Jesus, a great deal obviously hangs on our assessment of the reliability of the early church's oral tradition. Have form critics and legendary-Jesus theorists been correct in arguing that word-of-mouth transmission of information is inherently unreliable? Have their assumptions about oral traditions in the early church been correct? We shall now argue that recent research—particularly that associated with orality studies over the last several decades—strongly suggests that, as a matter of fact, each of these form critical assumptions is wrong.

The Likelihood of Writing in the Earliest Christian Communities

Form criticism has tended to embrace the view that, in all likelihood, neither Jesus nor anyone in his inner circle was literate. It was thus assumed that writing played no regulative role in the oral transmission of early material about Jesus, which made it easier for this material to be significantly and quickly altered as it was passed along. However, while no one disputes that first-century Jewish culture was an orally dominant culture, there is evidence that reading and writing were not as rare in the ancient Greco-Roman world in general, and in ancient Palestine in particular, as is often thought.[2]

For example, whereas some have argued that only the wealthy in the ancient world could have received the education needed to become literate, researchers have discovered clear evidence of writing among military personnel, slaves, and common laborers.[3] So too, whereas it was commonly assumed in the past that writing materials were very rare and expensive in the ancient world, we now have evidence that certain kinds of writing materials were actually rather inexpensive and were utilized by segments of the lower classes.[4] Archaeologists have also discovered texts that were intended to inform the general public (for example, publicly posted notices) that seem to presuppose some degree of literacy among the general populace.[5]

If the ancient world was, in general, more literate than commonly thought, we have reason to believe Jewish males would have been even more so. After all, as New Testament scholar John Meier notes, "The very identity and continued existence of the people of Israel were tied to a corpus of written and regularly read works in a way that simply was not true of other peoples in the Mediterranean world of the first-century. . . . To be able to read and explain the Scriptures was a revered goal for religiously minded Jews. Hence literacy held a special importance for the Jewish community."[6]

Thus, as Birger Gerhardsson argues, "The milieu in which Jesus and the original disciples ministered, and the milieu in which remembrances of Jesus' life and teaching were passed on, was one that revered the written word and thus valued literacy."[7]

In light of this, we have no reason to question the Gospels' portrayal of Jesus as not only being able to read (e.g., Luke 4:16–30), but as impressing crowds with his learning (e.g., John 7:15). Nor do we have any reason to suppose that all of Jesus's disciples were illiterate. At the very least, Matthew's occupation as a tax collector would have required some level of literacy. It is perhaps significant in this regard that an early second-century church father named Papias—a man who seems to have been in direct contact with the apostle John—mentions that Matthew was a designated note-taker among the earliest disciples.[8]

We thus conclude that, while the recollection of Jesus's words and deeds would have been passed on *primarily* by word of mouth in the early church, it seems more likely than not that, to some extent at least, they also would have been recorded in written forms. These written materials likely would have provided a check on how much the oral traditions about Jesus could have been altered over the first several decades within the newfound Christian communities.

Oral Traditions and Extended Narratives

One of the assumptions that is now being overturned in the discipline of orality studies is the longstanding idea that oral traditions are incapable of transmitting extended narratives. It was commonly assumed that long narratives simply would have been too difficult to remember to be passed on reliably. Countering this assumption, a large number of fieldwork studies over the last several decades have "brought to light numerous long oral epics in the living traditions of Central Asia, India, Africa, and Oceania, for example." Hence, argues folklore specialist Lauri Honko, "The existence of genuine long oral epics can no longer be denied."[9] In fact, oral narratives lasting up to twenty-five hours and requiring several days to perform have been documented![10] Indeed, oral performances—that is, times when the community's narrators (or tradents) pass on oral traditions to the community—almost always presuppose a broader narrative framework even when the entire narrative itself is not explicitly recounted in the particular performance.[11] There is, therefore, no longer any reason to suspect that the narrative framework of Jesus's life was the fictional creation of the Gospel authors.

Along these lines, it's interesting to compare the typical characteristics of oral performances with the Gospels. For example, specialists of oral traditions have discovered that oral performances are characterized by a balance between form and freedom. That is, the narrator is granted a certain amount of creativity and flexibility in how he or she presents the traditional material, but there are also strong constraints when it comes to altering the core content of traditional material. What specific material a tradent decides to include or exclude in any given oral performance and even, to some extent, the order in which the narrator decides to present traditional material in any given oral performance, depends largely on the needs, time constraints, and interests of the community at the time of the particular oral performance. But, again, if the narrator alters the material too much, the community objects and corrects him or her in the midst of the performance. In this way, the community itself serves an important custodial role in making sure its treasured oral traditions are not substantially altered by any single tradent or performance.

When one compares the Gospels and understands them in the context of the orally dominant culture in which they arose, one discovers this same sort of balance. The overall narrative framework and essential content of the portrait of Jesus we find in these texts is quite consistent, but there is also considerable freedom in how the material is presented. The order of events and wording of Jesus's sayings, for example, often varies from Gospel to Gospel, though the basic content and broad narrative framework is similar. In light of the new discoveries in orality studies, this suggests that we should view the Gospels as written versions—or "textualizations"—of the oral performances that would have been so common among the early Christian communities. And all of this suggests that the oral traditions about Jesus that lie behind the Gospels—including their overall narrative framework of his life—are solidly rooted in history.

Oral Traditions and Historical Concerns

As noted above, another common assumption that has driven much contemporary New Testament criticism over the last hundred years is that the early Christians had little interest in preserving historically accurate traditions about Jesus. Unfortunately for this view, another significant finding by specialists of religiously and/or historically oriented oral traditions over the last several decades has been that this assumption is unfounded.

The Tradent as Oral Historian

We now know that not only are orally oriented communities *capable* of cultivating historical concern, they *usually* embody a rather keen historical interest—particularly with respect to historically oriented traditions that are tied to the community's very self-identity. While "folklore is present," according to folklorist Richard Dorson, "so is historical content. . . . Even more importantly, so are historical attitudes of the tradition's bearers."[12] Anthropologist Patrick Pender-Cudlip goes so far as to argue that oral tradents typically have as much concern "to receive and render a precise, accurate and authentic account of the past" as do modern historians.[13]

Another orality expert, Joseph Miller, describes oral tradents as "professional historians in the sense that they are conscious of history and evidence." Hence, he adds, "Oral historians are . . . no less conscious of the past than are historians in literate cultures."[14] As a number of scholars have noted, oral tradents as well as the orally dominant communities they perform in consistently exhibit a keen capacity to distinguish historical fact from creative fiction.[15]

Indeed, as we've already noted, both the oral tradent and the community share a responsibility to guard the accuracy of the oral tradition, as evidenced by the fact that communities typically interrupt historically oriented oral performances if they discern the narrator getting something wrong. Because of this historical interest and the community's checks and balances, some experts in the field of oral traditions have gone so far as to argue that, at times, history preserved in orally dominant communities may actually be *more* reliable than history written down by elite individual historians in modern contexts.[16]

Given the remarkable consistency of certain characteristics of oral traditions and oral performances across a wide variety of cultures, we are justified in applying these insights to our understanding of oral traditions in the early church. And this means we have every reason to suppose that the earliest Christian communities would have been invested in preserving the historical accuracy of their traditional material about Jesus, including the essential narrative framework of his ministry.

Oral Tradition, History, and the Early Church

In fact, this much is clear from Paul's own writings. For example, Paul's letters reflect a deep concern with passing on established traditions (e.g., 1 Cor. 11:2, 23–26; 15:1–3; Gal. 1:9; Phil. 4:9; Col. 2:6–7; 1 Thess. 4:1; 2 Thess. 2:15; 3:6). Indeed, he places remarkable weight on these traditions. As Robert Stein notes, "Such traditions were to be 'held' on to (1 Cor. 15:1–2; 2 Thess. 2:15); life was to be lived 'in accord' with the tradition (2 Thess. 3:6; cf. Phil. 4:9), for the result of this would be salvation (1 Cor. 15:1–2), whereas its rejection meant damnation (Gal. 1:9). The reason for this view was that this tradition had God himself as its ultimate source (1 Cor. 11:23)."[17]

This incredible emphasis on tradition explains why early Christianity stressed the importance of "teachers" (e.g., Acts 13:1; Rom. 12:7; 1 Cor. 12:28–29; Eph. 4:11; Heb. 5:12; James 3:1; *Didache* 15:1–2). In a predominantly oral community such as the early church, the primary function of these teachers would have been to faithfully transmit the oral traditions.[18]

There are a host of other indications that the early church shared the typical concern of orally dominant communities with accurately preserving the essential elements of their oral traditions. For example, James Dunn notes the prevalent themes of "bearing witness" to Jesus (e.g., John 1:7–8, 15, 19, 32, 34; 3:26, 28; 5:32; Acts 1:8, 22; 2:32; 3:15; 5:32; 10:37–41; 13:31; 22:15, 18; 23:11; 26:16) and to "remembering" the ministry, death, and resurrection of Jesus within the early church (Luke 22:19; 1 Cor. 11:2, 24–25; 2 Thess. 2:5; 2 Tim. 2:8, 14). This hardly suggests a community that has little interest in accurate history![19] So too, it's significant that both Paul and Luke (in the book of Acts) depict the apostles as providing links of continuity between the church and Jesus, with special emphasis being given to Peter, John, and James the brother of Jesus (e.g., Acts 1:15, 21–22; 2:14, 42; 3:1–11; 4:13, 19; 5:1–10, 15, 29; 8:14; 12:2; 1 Cor. 15:1–8; Gal. 2:9; Eph. 2:20).

For all these reasons we conclude that, contrary to the assumption that the early Christians had little interest in preserving historical accuracy, the early church from the beginning had a rather intense historical interest in the life, death, and resurrection of Jesus.

The Crucial Role of Eyewitnesses

Finally, we must discuss the common assumption that oral traditions are derived primarily from the felt needs of the community and are not anchored in the experience of individual eyewitnesses. This assumption has fueled the classic form critical view that the Jesus story was largely originated and shaped to address ongoing needs in the early Jesus movement. Related to this, it has fueled the view that individual eyewitnesses of Jesus's life would have played little or no role in originating or regulating oral traditions about Jesus. Here, too, research into certain religiously oriented oral traditions and orally dominant communities—as well as clear evidence from the early Jesus tradition itself—exposes a classic form critical assumption to be mistaken.

The Tradition Bearer

Orality specialists now realize that, while the community plays a significant role in preserving the accuracy of an oral tradition, as we've seen, oral communities typically designate individual tradents—or "strong tradition bearers"—to be the primary and official transmitters of the tradition.[20] When an individual was an eyewitness to events that have become part a community's oral historical traditions, he or she is often recognized as a crucial link in the communal preservation of that tradition.[21]

This new research sheds important light on our understanding of the oral Jesus tradition. If the oral period of the early church functioned similarly to the way we now know oral communities tend to operate, we should expect that those individuals who were closest to Jesus during his ministry would have played a significant role in the transmission of oral material about Jesus. Certainly the traditional material was shaped by the needs of the early faith communities because, as we have seen, oral tradents always shape their performances according to the particular situation of their audience. But this discovery of the crucial role of individual tradents suggests that we can no longer conceive of the traditional material about Jesus being transmitted in the early church *apart from the strong influence of original eyewitnesses.* This renders it virtually impossible to conceive of the oral traditions in the early church veering too far from the historical events observed by eyewitnesses.

Authoritative Eyewitnesses and the Early Church

The point is strongly reinforced when we recall that early Christianity was a thoroughly Jewish movement, for the Jewish tradition had always put a strong emphasis on the role of eyewitnesses. Only by appealing to credible eyewitnesses could one certify a claim as factual (e.g., Ruth 4:9–11; Isa. 8:1–2; Jer. 32:10–12). So too, bearing false witness was considered a major crime. Indeed, it was outlawed in the Ten Commandments (Exod. 20:16). The law of multiple witnesses also reflects the life-or-death importance of this command in ancient Judaism (Num. 35:30; Deut. 17:6–7).

This emphasis on the importance of eyewitnesses was quite explicitly carried over into the early church. The Mosaic law regarding multiple witnesses was appealed to within the Jesus community (Mark 14:56, 59; John 5:31–32; Heb. 10:28) and was made the basis of church discipline (Matt. 18:16; 2 Cor. 13:1; 1 Tim. 5:19). More broadly, the themes of bearing witness, giving a true testimony, and making a true confession are everywhere present in the tradition of the early church (e.g., Matt. 10:17; Mark 6:11; 13:9–13; Luke 1:1–2; 9:5; 21:12; 22:71; John 1:7–8, 15, 19, 32, 34).[22] As Robert Stein observes, the sheer pervasiveness of these themes in the early church testifies to "the high regard in which eyewitness testimony was held."[23] It also explains the previously noted high regard given to certain individuals in the early church (e.g., Peter, James, John) for their role as witnesses, teachers, and preservers of the Jesus tradition (e.g., Acts 1:15, 21–22; 2:14, 42; 3:1–11; 4:13, 19; 5:1–10, 15, 29; 8:14; 12:2; 1 Cor. 15:1–8; Gal. 2:9; Eph. 2:20). All of this is what we should expect, given that the early church was a thoroughly Jewish, orally dominated culture.

Conclusion

To summarize, it seems we have every reason to conclude that the oral traditions about Jesus in the early church were passed on in a generally reliable fashion. Notes taken during Jesus's ministry would have constrained the extent to which these traditions would have evolved. But, even more significantly, everything we're learning about oral traditions in orally dominant cultures suggests that the earliest Jesus communities would have cared about the historicity of their traditional material and would have been quite capable of preserving the essential historicity of their traditions. And this, of course, is not good news for any who insist that the Gospels' portrait of Jesus is largely, if not entirely, legendary.

We have thus far shown that major lines of argumentation used to claim that the Gospels' portrait of Jesus is substantially legendary rather than substantially historical do not succeed. In part 2 we turn to evaluate the historicity of the Gospels themselves.

PART TWO

The Gospels and Ten Tests
of Historical Reliability

I n part 1 we argued that there is no intellectual justification for ruling out the possibility that miracles can, on occasion, happen (chapter 1); first-century Jewish culture was a most unlikely context for a myth or legend to arise about a man being the embodiment of Yahweh (chapter 2); there are no compelling reasons to think Paul viewed Jesus along the lines of ancient mystery religions (chapter 3); none of the alleged parallels to the Jesus story succeed in showing it to be a myth or legend (chapter 4); and the crucial assumptions made by classical form critics, assumptions that led many to doubt the essential veracity of the early church's oral traditions, were wrong (chapter 5). On these grounds we have rather compelling reasons to think it more probable than not that the portrait of Jesus presented in the Gospels is, to say the least, generally reliable.

In part 2 we shall argue that this case grows much stronger as we consider the Gospels themselves. When evaluated by the same criteria critical historians typically use to evaluate ancient documents, the Gospels give us many reasons to conclude that the image of Jesus they present is historically reliable. In this second half of our book, therefore, we shall submit the Gospels to ten tests critical historians typically apply to ancient documents as they test their historical reliability.[1]

First, historians must ask of an ancient document, Do we possess copies of the work that are reasonably close to the original? It hardly makes sense to try to assess an ancient document's historical reliability if we aren't sure what the ancient document originally claimed. Second, historians inquire into whether the author of the work *intended* to communicate reliable history. Clearly, if there are literary signals that a work didn't intend to report reliable history, there are good grounds for doubting its ostensive historical claims. We submit the Gospels to these two tests in chapter 6.

Third, historians are interested in determining whether an author was in a position to accurately record the history he or she claims to report. Fourth, historians attempt to discern the biases an author brought to his or her work and the extent to which this bias distorted the historical reporting. We'll explore these two issues as they pertain to the Gospels in chapter 7.

Fifth, historians typically investigate documents to determine whether they incorporate the kind of details and textual signals that tend to accompany reports that are rooted in eyewitness testimony. Sixth, historians are particularly interested in whether an ancient work incorporates material that is "self-damaging"—that is, material that works counter to any bias the author seems to have—and thus historically rooted material one might have expected the writer to leave out. In chapter 8 we'll submit the Gospels to these two tests.

Seventh, historians always want to know whether a document is self-consistent or consistent with other works that purport to report the same events as the document they are examining. This is an especially important issue with regard to the Gospels, since here we have essentially the same story told from four different perspectives. Eighth, critical historians question whether the events recorded in an ancient work are intrinsically believable or unbelievable. We'll explore how the Gospels fare under these two criteria in chapter 9.

Ninth, scholars typically attempt to discover whether there's any literary evidence that, while perhaps not reporting on all of the same events as the document they're examining (as in the seventh criterion above), nevertheless provides information that impacts their assessment of that document. In chapter 10, therefore, we'll investigate first- and second-century references to Jesus found outside the canonical Gospels.

Finally, historians want to know if there are any archaeological findings that either confirm or stand in tension with claims made by the document they're examining. While ancient archaeological evidence tends to be sparse as well as controversial inasmuch as it is often open to a variety of interpretations, in chapter 11 we'll look at twelve findings, or sets of findings, that arguably confirm aspects of the Gospels.

We'll conclude this work in chapter 12 by exploring the relationship the Jesus story has to legend and myth. We'll argue that, while we've no reason to judge the Jesus story to be legendary or mythological, we have many reasons to believe it fulfills the essential dream that lies behind a good many legendary and mythic stories. Indeed, we'll argue that the way the Jesus story fulfills the impulse behind all good legends and myths gives us one more reason for concluding that it is rooted in history.

6

Following the Paper Trail

The Questions of Textual Reconstruction, Literary Genre, and Historical Intent

As we have noted, there are ten questions critical historians commonly ask as they attempt to determine the historical veracity of any ancient document. In this chapter we address the first two of these questions.[1]

Question 1: Do we possess copies of the work that are reasonably close to the original?

Before we can assess the historical veracity of an ancient work, we first need to be confident that the work we possess is a reasonably close representation of the original. Since texts had to be copied by hand prior to the invention of the printing press in the fifteenth century, and since we know this method of disseminating texts is prone to error, this is a very important consideration. Scholars known as "textual critics" collect and compare available fragmentary or whole versions of an ancient work along with any extant quotations of the work by other ancient sources in order to reconstruct, as much as possible, the original text of the document in question.

So, how do the Gospels fare on this matter? It's no exaggeration to say that if ever we have reason to be confident we possess copies of an ancient work that are reasonably close to the original, it is with the Gospels. These works, together with the whole New Testament, have far better textual attestation than any other ancient work.

We possess roughly 5,500 ancient Greek manuscripts of the New Testament, either in fragments or in whole.[2] On top of this, we possess thousands of ancient translations of the New Testament as well as countless citations by early Christian writers.[3] By comparison, among the next best attested ancient works is Homer's *Iliad*, for which we have less than seven hundred published manuscripts. Among the Greek tragedies, the most abundant in extant manuscripts are those of Euripides, which number less than four hundred. In terms of ancient historical works, we possess nine Greek manuscripts of Josephus's *Jewish War*, about twenty manuscripts of Livy's Roman history, ten good manuscripts of Caesar's *Gallic War*, and one ninth-century manuscript of a portion of Tacitus's *Annals* (books I–VI).[4] Obviously, the New Testament is in a class by itself in terms of the wealth of our textual attestation.

Equally relevant is the relatively early dating of some of these manuscripts. Our earliest fragment of a Gospel text comes from the first half of the second century.[5] Over twenty papyri containing portions of one or more of the Gospels can be dated to the third and fourth centuries. Five virtually complete texts of the New Testament date from the fourth and fifth centuries. In fact, even if we possessed no ancient copies of the New Testament, we could reproduce most of it simply by consulting the many quotations within the works of the church fathers in the first three centuries. No other ancient work comes close to this wealth of early textual attestation. For example, the earliest copy of Homer's *Iliad* we possess dates approximately nine hundred years after the original—and that is remarkably good by ancient standards. In most cases the earliest copies of ancient works date more than a thousand years after the original.[6]

A third important consideration involves the geographical distribution of a text. In general, the wider the distribution of an ancient manuscript, the greater the likelihood of discovering independent lines of witness. As textual critics identify various textual "families," comparing these independent families can bring to light copying variations. The relatively early spread of New Testament texts throughout the Mediterranean world offers a remarkable geographical distribution and diversity with which to work. In fact, here too the New Testament has far and away better attestation than any other ancient manuscript. Clearly, if anyone is going to doubt that the copies of the Gospels we possess today are reasonably close to the originals, they would have to reject outright the textual reliability of virtually every other ancient text.

Question 2: The Genre Question—Did the author intend to report reliable history?

Obviously, if a document wasn't written for the purpose of reporting history, we'd be misguided in expecting it to do so. Did the authors of the Gospels intend their works to be read as, among other things, reliable accounts of the life of Jesus?

As we have seen, some of those who argue that the Jesus of the Gospels is substantially legendary believe the authors of the Gospels intentionally fabricated much (if not all) of their historical narrative about Jesus. What interests us presently is that some of these scholars go further and maintain that these authors *intended* their works *to be read* as fiction. We maintain that there are insurmountable problems with this view.

There are a number of different proposals as to what kind of fiction the Gospels were allegedly intended to be—a fact that already makes one wonder how solid the case is for any one of these suggestions. For our present purposes, however, it will suffice to discuss and critique two proposals that seem to be getting a good deal of attention these days. Our response to these two theories is along the lines we would give to any version of the Gospels-as-fiction thesis.

Mark as an Inspiring, Homeric Myth

One version of the Gospel-as-fiction thesis that seems to be gaining some credence in certain scholarly circles comes from Jesus Seminar member Dennis MacDonald.[7] MacDonald argues that the Gospel of Mark, upon which he believes Matthew and Luke are based, was intended to be an inspiring myth intentionally modeled after Homer's *Iliad* and *Odyssey*. The main reason MacDonald comes to this conclusion is that he claims to find significant parallels between Mark and Homer. We find at least six notable difficulties with MacDonald's thesis.

1. The parallels MacDonald finds between Mark and Homer strike us (and many others) as tenuous at best. For example, MacDonald argues that Mark's account of Jesus's mountaintop transfiguration (Mark 9:2–10) is modeled after Odysseus's revelation of his identity to Telemachus, for both scenes involve the revelation of someone's identity and both scenes involve shining clothing. But surely these two facts don't plausibly establish an intentional parallel.

If one suspects that Mark is paralleling another account at this point, one would think the episode of Moses receiving the Ten Commandments on Mount Sinai would be a more reasonable candidate. After all, the Gospel of Mark was written from within a first-century Jewish worldview that was centered on the Old Testament, not a pagan worldview that found great significance in Homer. Not only this, but Mark's transfiguration narrative has more in common with this account than with Odysseus's demonstration of his identity to Telemachus. Some have argued that the majority of alleged parallels MacDonald finds between Mark and Homer are more clearly paralleled in the Old Testament.[8]

2. Even if one grants that Mark significantly parallels Homer—or any other source, for that matter—this doesn't establish that Mark intentionally modeled his accounts on Homer or any other source. Samuel Sandmel appropriately labels the tendency to speculate about historical influence on the basis of perceived—but unwarranted—parallels as "parallelomania."[9] In reality, the commonalities may be due to the fact that Mark (or any other author under consideration) is steeped in a broader common tradition that influences the way he expresses his historical remembrances. Or perhaps certain commonalities may be due to the fact that different authors tap into mythic archetypes as they create their material or recite historical remembrances (see chapter 12). At the same time, many commonalities may simply be coincidental.

3. Closely related to this, MacDonald never adequately explains why Mark would create a theological fiction patterned after a Greek epic. More specifically, how could Mark have imagined that his largely Jew-

ish Christian audience would have found anything attractive, let alone compelling, with a Jesus modeled after a pagan character, let alone one as flawed as Odysseus? If this work was meant to be an inspiring myth, one can imagine much more inspiring characters Mark could have latched onto—for example, characters found in the Jewish Scriptures that both Mark and his audience were steeped in.

4. Even more fundamentally, it is not clear what Mark's supposed inspiring myth was meant to inspire people to believe and do. It is important to consider that most scholars date Mark soon after the great persecution of AD 64, when Nero attempted to eradicate the Christian movement in Rome through torture and execution. Beyond that, Christians had been, and continued to be, a rather despised group by both Jews and Romans throughout the empire. How is this compatible with the idea that Mark intended his work to be understood as a fiction? Who is willing to be persecuted—and possibly executed—for what is known to be a fictional tale?

5. If Mark was intentionally writing fiction, one has to wonder why *no one in the history of the church has read it as such*—including, it seems, Matthew and Luke, who presumably used Mark's work as the basis for their own Gospels. MacDonald argues that "readers for two thousand years apparently have been blind" to the fact that Mark was writing a fictional "prose anti-epic of sorts."[10] Are we really to believe that everyone got it wrong until MacDonald? This point is especially damaging to MacDonald's theory because he leverages a good bit on the claim that Mark's original audience *would have* picked up on textual clues that indicate his account is a Homeric-styled myth, not a work that intends to communicate true history.[11] Unfortunately for MacDonald's thesis, it seems that *none* of Mark's contemporaries read it this way!

6. MacDonald asks us to believe that Mark was a rather savvy, sophisticated writer who could have expected his audience to pick up subtle parallels between his text and those of Homer (even though, as we just said, it seems none of his audience did). Another significant problem with this thesis, however, is that it is quite out of sync with what we know about the role that writing plays in the sort of orally dominant contexts that would have characterized the early Christian movement.

We modern Western people live in what can be called a "literary paradigm" that is very different from the "oral paradigm" of ancient people living in an orally dominant culture. Among other things, we tend to imagine writers consciously and closely interacting with other texts they have in front of them as they compose their works. We also tend to imagine them writing for audiences who silently read their works in private and are informed by other texts that they, again, silently read in private. If orality studies have demonstrated anything over the last several decades, however, it is that this is not at all how writing functions in cultures where reading and writing play a less dominant role. In these cultures, writing is generally an extension of oral communication and thus does not presuppose most of the features that characterize modern writing. Written texts in oral environments are written to be heard in a communal context, usually in one sitting, not silently and meticulously studied in private. As some experts put it, they are written with an oral rather than literary "register."[12]

In this light, MacDonald's contention that the original hearers of Mark would have picked up subtle interactions with Homer's work (which was also written to be communally heard, not privately studied) must be judged to be quite unlikely. MacDonald is anachronistically reading a modern, literary paradigm into ancient, orally orientated texts. Or, to put it differently, he is reading these texts as though they were written with a literary rather than an oral "register."

The Gospels as Midrash

A second rather popular version of the Gospels-as-fiction proposal holds that the Gospels are a form of Jewish midrash. While scholars debate a number of issues surrounding the exact definition of *midrash*, for our purposes we can think of it simply as an ancient way of interpreting Scripture to make it relevant in the contemporary setting.[13] One way this was done was by retelling a biblical story as though it was a contemporary event. Another way was by creatively applying Old Testament texts to contemporary events, claiming, for example, that the contemporary event fulfilled these Old Testament texts.

Almost all New Testament scholars acknowledge that the authors of the Gospels use *midrashic techniques* within their works. For example, when Jesus, Mary, and Joseph flee from Herod into Egypt, it is said this happened to fulfill what was written, "Out of Egypt I have called my son" (Matt. 2:15). As is common with midrash, if you read the passage Mathew is alluding to (Hosea 11:1), you'll find there's absolutely nothing predictive or messianic about it. Yahweh is simply referring to the fact that he called the *nation of Israel* out of Egypt.

Matthew, of course, knew this, as would every Jewish person who read Matthew's Gospel. We thus can't imagine Matthew thinking he could pull the wool over the eyes of his audience in the hope that they would think this Old Testament verse actually *predicted* that the Messiah would go into and come out of Egypt (though this is the way some misguided Christian apologists today interpret these "fulfillment passages"). Rather, Matthew is simply contemporizing the Exodus for (mostly Jewish) Christians of his day—demonstrating the ongoing significance of Scripture in light of more current acts of God in history. In this way he is also bringing out an aspect of Jesus's significance for these Christians, suggesting, it seems, that Jesus embodies (fulfills) the significance of Israel. Something similar could be said for many of the Old Testament passages that the four Gospel authors say Jesus fulfilled.

So let's grant that the Gospel authors, at times, use some form of midrashic interpretive technique. But the view that the Gospels *are* midrash goes far beyond this, for this view holds that the Jesus portrayed in these works is, at least to a significant degree, a *midrashic fiction*. According to this view, Gospel authors not only updated the Old Testament in light of Jesus; the Gospel authors fabricated a portrait of Jesus on the basis of what they found in the Old Testament.

Regarding Matthew 2:15, for example, this view wouldn't say that Matthew merely reinterpreted Hosea *in light of* the fact that Jesus spent several years in Egypt. Rather, it would hold that Matthew *fabricated* Jesus's family fleeing into Egypt and then coming out of Egypt precisely so Jesus would fulfill Hosea 11:1. Some defenders of this view go so far as to argue we have no reason to think an actual person named Jesus even existed.[14]

The Gospels-as-midrash thesis is certainly provocative, but there are at least five fundamental problems with it.

1. The idea that the Jesus of the Gospels is entirely a midrashic fiction hinges on our accepting that Paul and his mid-first-century congregations viewed Jesus as a mythic savior figure who came to earth in the distant past. If Christians at the time of Paul's writing believed that Jesus lived

only two decades earlier, that his mother, brother, and original disciples were yet living among them, and the like, it is hard to imagine the Gospel authors fabricating an entirely different Jesus several decades later and impossible to imagine Christians broadly accepting such a fabrication even if certain authors had created one. Unfortunately for the Gospels-as-midrash view, we have very good reasons to conclude that Paul and all mid-first-century Christians viewed Jesus as a recent contemporary, as we have seen (chapter 3). Neither Paul nor the earliest Christians for whom he wrote viewed Jesus as a mythical cosmic savior figure who lived and redeemed the world "long, long ago and far, far away."

2. As David Brewer has established in his exhaustive study of first-century Jewish interpretive techniques, this method of biblical interpretation was counterbalanced by a more literal interpretive paradigm. Throughout the first century, traditional scribes tended to practice a much more sober mode of exegesis.[15] While we can easily imagine the Gospel authors *using* midrash to some degree, there is also evidence of this countertendency at work in the Gospels. Thus, there is no warrant for claiming that these authors created a fictional midrashic Jesus.

3. While ancient Jewish exegetes sometimes used midrash to correlate current historical events with Old Testament texts, we have no clear examples of them *making up* current events to fulfill Old Testament texts. Yet this is precisely what the defenders of the Gospels-as-midrash thesis are claiming the Gospel authors did. This seriously undermines the plausibility of this theory.

4. If the Gospel authors were going to fabricate a midrashic Jesus, one would have thought he would have better conformed to first-century Jewish expectations of what the Messiah was supposed to be. Far from meeting the social and religious expectations of most first-century Jews about the Messiah, however, the Gospels' portraits of Jesus are *offensive* to these social and religious expectations, as we shall discuss more fully in chapter 8. The surprising, countercultural features of the Gospels' portraits of Jesus can only be adequately explained if we accept that Jesus was, as a matter of historical fact, a surprisingly countercultural Messiah figure.

5. Finally, if the Gospel authors had engaged in the activity of creating portraits of the Messiah on the basis of a midrashic interpretation of the Old Testament, one wonders why their use of the Old Testament is, quite

frankly, often quite awkward. For example, John depicts the episode of a guard giving Jesus "sour wine" as a fulfillment of Psalm 69, in which David complains that his enemies "gave me poison for food, and for my thirst they gave me vinegar to drink" (Ps. 69:21; cf. John 19:28–29). We have to seriously wonder why any first-century author would choose to create a fictitious episode in the life of a mostly (if not entirely) fictitious messiah on the basis of this obscure verse in the first place. Why did this verse, which has nothing predictive about it, jump out at John as a candidate for John's revision of Jesus?

Moreover, if John was attempting to create an episode in Jesus's life to fulfill this verse, why did he have Jesus receive sour wine instead of vinegar? More baffling still, why did he have Jesus fulfill the *last half* of the sentence *but not the first half*? If John was fabricating the account in a midrashic fashion, why did he not also depict Jesus being given poison for food?

So far as we can see, the only way to explain John's peculiar use of this obscure passage is by assuming that John's exegesis *was driven by actual events in Jesus's life*. If, as a matter of historical fact, Jesus was actually given sour wine when he asked for water, we can begin to understand why John found something significant about the second half of an otherwise obscure sentence in the Old Testament that refers to David being given vinegar for water. In light of what actually happened to Jesus, John was able to relate it to David's experience in Psalm 69, thereby highlighting a significant moment of Jesus's life for his audience. He was, it seems, saying that Jesus embodies the sort of mistreatment God's servants (like David) have often undergone. Indeed, in an important sense, Jesus, the true Davidic king, completes the mistreatment David himself experienced. *In this sense David anticipates Jesus, and Jesus fulfills David*. But if John is instead creating an episode in Jesus's life on the basis of this verse, his partial and strange use of this obscure verse is utterly unintelligible.

We could argue in a similar fashion about many of the Old Testament passages Jesus is said to fulfill in the Gospels. Given what actually happened to Jesus, the authors' midrashic use of the Old Testament makes sense (at least by ancient Jewish standards). But if we instead suppose the Gospel authors fabricated a Jesus on the basis of the Old Testament, as the Gospels-as-midrash advocates ask us to do, we are left with some inexplicable problems.

The Genre Debate and the Historical Intent of the Gospels

In light of all this, it seems clear that the Gospels were not written to be read as fiction. Rather, among other things, they were intended to communicate events in history. What is not so clear, however, is exactly what kind of literary genre the authors intended their Gospels to be, and there is a good deal of scholarly debate about this.

Some scholars argue that the Gospels—especially Luke—come closest to the genre of ancient historiography similar to Josephus, Livy, Thucydides, Tacitus, and others. Others argue that the Gospels are better understood as examples of ancient biographies. This genre differed from ancient histories primarily in the fact that it tended to focus on one exemplary life rather than on a broader history, and it tended to include more anecdotal material than historical writings. Others argue that the lines between these two genres were so blurred in the ancient world that we're thinking anachronistically if we try to reductively force the Gospels into one or the other. And still others argue that the Gospels do not fit neatly into *any* ancient genre: they are *sui generis* in nature.

It is our contention that the Gospel genre is, in some respects, quite similar to ancient biography, though not purely reducible to it. Likewise, the Gospels show clear evidence of historical intent, though without being reducible to ancient historiography per se. In important ways, the Gospels represent a distinct genre, particularly with respect to their subject matter. What is important to note for our purposes here —regardless of where one comes out on the Gospel genre debate—is that, among other things, the Gospel authors show clear signs of intending to pass on historically reliable data about Jesus. As Gregory Dawes perceptively notes, the Gospel authors "do seem to have taken for granted the historical reality of the events they narrate. More seriously, their theological message is built upon this assumption of historical factuality. The interpreter who wishes to respect the evangelists' intentions may not simply set aside, as theologically irrelevant, the question of the historicity of these stories."[16]

As we will explore in more depth below, the Gospel authors communicate this historical intention in ways that are quite fitting for an orally dominant culture. Thus, when properly understood in their ancient context, their *historical intent* is undeniable.

7

Who, When, and Why?

The Questions of Historical Position and Bias

W e turn now to apply to the Gospels two more questions historians typically ask of ancient documents as they attempt to discern their historical reliability.[1]

Question 3: Were the authors of the gospels in a position to write reliable history?

Historians want to know whether an ancient author was in a position to know what he or she was talking about. Obviously, it is best if the author was an eyewitness of the events he or she records, but this is rather rare in history. The next best thing is for the author to have been in direct contact with eyewitnesses, though that too is not common. Usually historians are content if the author was indirectly in contact with eyewitnesses through oral or written sources. Since information tends to get distorted as it is passed on, whether in written or oral form, the closer the author is to the events he or she records, the more trustworthy the report is considered to be, all other things being equal. We will now investigate how well the Gospels fare under these criteria.

The Orality Argument

Legendary-Jesus scholars, among others, usually argue that we don't know who wrote the Gospels. The names now associated with them were added later, and they argue that early church tradition on this subject is not reliable. Moreover, while more conservative scholars tend to date various Gospels twenty to forty years after Jesus lived, more liberal scholars tend to date them forty to seventy years after his life.

We shall shortly argue that the case for accepting the early church tradition regarding the authorship and relatively early dating of the four Gospels is stronger than many suppose. But first we want to suggest that not too much hangs on this. That is, even if we grant that the Gospels were written between AD 70 and 100, as many scholars maintain, and even if we grant that we don't know who wrote these works, this *still* doesn't warrant the conclusion that these authors were not in a position to pass on reliable history.

In this regard it's important to recall from chapter 5 three things that recent orality studies have taught us. First, orally dominant communities typically are invested in accurately preserving the memory of events that shape their communal identity. They have genuine historical concerns. Second, while tradents entrusted with the task of retelling a community's oral traditions are allowed creative flexibility in how they express traditional material, the community as a whole typically assumes responsibility to ensure that the tradent's creative performance doesn't alter the substance of the tradition he or she is passing on. So it is, as many orality specialists now argue, that orally dominant communities typically evidence the ability to reliably transmit historical material for long periods of time—in some cases, for centuries. And third, the role of writing in orally dominant communities is not to express an individual's novel perspectives on some matter (such as it is with modern writing) but, as with oral performances, to recall and creatively re-express the community's tradition. They are written with an oral rather than a literary register.

Putting these three considerations together, it should be clear that, *whoever they were and whenever they wrote*, we have reasons to accept that the Gospel authors were in a position to transmit reliable reports about Jesus. Unless we arbitrarily assume that the early Christian communities were remarkably atypical for orally dominant communities, the sheer fact that the Gospel authors wrote as tradents of an early church tradition should incline us to accept this much. Had these authors expressed a vision of Jesus that was substantially inconsistent with the church's oral tradition, the community never would have accepted them. And as we've argued (chapter 5), there is no reason to think the early Christian community's orally transmitted vision of Jesus would have substantially morphed in the time prior to the writing of these works. Indeed, sixty years is not a significant stretch of time by the standards of oral traditions. In fact, within this time frame, it is more likely that we are dealing with "oral history" rather than "oral tradition" per se.[2]

A Comparison with Other Historical Sources

It is perhaps worth mentioning at this point that historians frequently trust ancient authors who wrote about events that preceded them by greater spans of time than forty to sixty years and who were not directly connected to the events they wrote about via a community's orally transmitted history. For example, much of what historians believe we know about first-century Jewish history comes from a single source—Josephus—writing about events that in some cases predate him by more than a century. So too, much of what historians believe we know about the Persian wars comes from a single source—Herodotus—writing roughly seventy years after the fact. And a good deal of what we think we know about Alexander the Great comes from a single source—Arrian—writing roughly four centuries after Alexander lived.

Of course, historians don't uncritically trust these sources. They apply to these ancient works the other sort of criteria we're discussing, as they do to all ancient documents (and as we are doing to the Gospels). But, unless they're given reason to think otherwise on particular matters, historians accept these sources as being *generally* reliable. Why should we then assume a more skeptical stance toward the Gospel authors? They wrote closer to the events they record than these other writers did, and they wrote as tradents within an orally dominant community that was invested in preserving the memory of the events they record.

This much is true even if we grant that the Gospels are anonymous and late. But we shall now argue that there is no compelling reason to grant this much. True, as was quite typical of works in the ancient world, the authors of the Gospels didn't identify themselves in their works. But, as we shall now see, their authorship was attested by a number of early sources, and we see no compelling reason to think these sources were mistaken.

The Tradition of Authorship of the Gospels

The Gospel of Mark. The first reference we have to the author of the Gospel of Mark comes from Papias, an early second-century Christian and acquaintance of the apostle John, who says that John passed on to him the following tradition:

> Mark became Peter's interpreter and wrote accurately all that he remembered, not, indeed, in order, of the things said or done by the Lord. For he had not heard the Lord, nor followed him, but later on, as I said, followed Peter, who used to give teachings as necessity demanded but not making, as it were, an arrangement of the Lord's oracles, so that Mark did nothing wrong in thus writing down single points as he remembered them. For to one thing he gave attention, to leave out nothing of what he had heard and to make no false statements in them.[3]

The report that Mark took notes from Peter and composed the Gospel that bears his name is subsequently confirmed by Irenaeus, Tertullian, and Clement of Alexandria.[4]

The Gospel of Matthew. Regarding Matthew, Eusebius records a statement of Papias's that says that Matthew wrote down the sayings of the Lord and that others translated or interpreted them as best they could.[5] It's not at all clear that Papias is referring to the Gospel of Matthew, but this remark at least demonstrates that Matthew was known in the early church as a writer, making the traditional authorship of the Gospel of Matthew somewhat more probable.

Irenaeus, writing around AD 180, attests the traditional authorship of Matthew in a more direct way when he writes, "Now Matthew published among the Hebrews in their own tongue also a written Gospel, while Peter and Paul were preaching in Rome and founding the church."[6] So too, Eusebius records Origen as stating that Matthew, the erstwhile tax collector and apostle, wrote the first Gospel in the language of the Jews.[7]

The Gospel of Luke. The earliest confirmation we have of the authorship of this Gospel also comes from Irenaeus, who noted that a heretic named Marcion "mutilates this Gospel which is according to Luke, removes all that is written respecting the generation of the Lord, and sets aside a great deal of the teaching of the Lord's discourses in which the Lord is recorded as most clearly confessing that the creator of the universe is his Father."[8]

Eusebius later records Irenaeus as saying, "Luke also who was a follower of Paul put down in a book the gospel that was preached by him."[9] The *Anti-Marcionite Prologue*, probably written toward the end of the second century, offers yet more information: "Luke is a Syrian of Antioch, a Syrian by race, a physician by profession. He had become a disciple of the apostles and later followed Paul until his (Paul's) martyrdom, having served the Lord continuously, unmarried, without children, filled with the Holy Spirit he died at the age of eighty-four years in Boeotia."[10]

The Gospel of John. Finally, regarding John, while Tatian, Claudius Apollinaris, and Athenagorus all quote the Gospel of John, no one explicitly identifies John as the author until Theophilus of Antioch around AD 180. About the same time, Irenaeus writes that "John the disciple of the Lord, who leaned back on his breast, published the Gospel while he was resident at Ephesus in Asia."[11] Eusebius reports that Clement of Alexandria taught that "Last of all, aware that the physical facts had been recorded in the gospels, encouraged by his pupils and irresistibly moved by the Spirit, John wrote a spiritual gospel."[12]

In Defense of the Traditional Authorship Claims

What are we to make of these testimonies? In our opinion, they are quite significant. What is most impressive about them, we believe, is that we have no record of anyone disputing them. Christians in the second and third centuries questioned the authorship of *other* works, but never *these*. This uniformity of opinion is more difficult to explain if the authorship of these works was inaccurately applied to them long after they'd been in circulation than if the authorship was attached to them from the start.[13]

Not only this, but as Martin Hengel has argued, a variety of practical issues in the early church would have prevented these documents from circulating anonymously for very long.[14] If their authorship wasn't acknowledged from the start, it had to have been assigned early on—and so the names associated with each work are more likely to be accurate than if this assigning had taken place long after the works had been in circulation. We also need to keep in mind that Christians of this time were frequently suffering persecution, and martyrdom was not uncommon. These early Christians would therefore have had more than an academic interest in knowing who wrote these works upon which they were staking their lives.

On top of all this, it's difficult to explain why these works were so quickly and so uniformly accepted as authoritative in the early church unless they were from the start associated with people within Jesus's inner circle (such as Matthew and John) or people close to this inner circle (such as Mark via Peter and Luke via Paul). Along these same lines, if prestigious names were fictitiously associated with these works to give them authority, as many scholars argue, how do we explain the traditional authorship of the Gospel of Mark and the Gospel of Luke? Wouldn't one have thought that someone like Peter or James would have been chosen before the relatively unknown persons of Mark and Luke?

On the basis of considerations like this, some scholars argue that it is more probable than not that the traditional authorship claims regarding the canonical Gospels is rooted in history. And this means we have good grounds for accepting that the Gospels were written at a relatively early date, either by eyewitnesses (Matthew and John) or by people working in close proximity with eyewitnesses (Mark and Luke). Indeed, even apart from the question of authorship, some scholars find grounds for dating all the Gospels before AD 70 and Mark perhaps as early as AD 40 to 50.[15]

In summary, while we don't *need* to accept the traditional authorship and early dating of these works to believe they were in a position to pass on reliable history, the evidence that they were written by the authors attested by the early church tradition and at a relatively early date only strengthens the case for their trustworthiness.

Question 4: To what degree does the author's bias compromise the document's reliability?

We turn now to the question of how the bias of the Gospel authors affected their works. Obviously, determining the extent to which an author's biases and agendas distort his or her reports is crucial to evaluating the author's historical trustworthiness. No one disputes that the Gospel authors were in fact biased. They were not trying to give a disinterested, objective account of Jesus's life. Rather, the Gospels were written by passionate devotees to help people "believe that Jesus is the Messiah, the Son of God," so that "through believing [they] may have life in his name" (John 20:31). In other words, they were evangelists, not academic historians.

Not only this, but beyond their shared, general bias as Christian evangelists, each Gospel author has his own distinct biases. Through the discipline known as "redaction criticism" scholars have demonstrated that each author tends to shape his material in particular ways. For example, assuming that Matthew and Luke both used Mark in composing their Gospels, as the majority of scholars hold, it seems pretty clear that Matthew tended to soften Mark's material, editing out potentially offensive features. To give one illustration, while Mark admits that Jesus *could not* perform many miracles in his hometown (Mark 6:5), Matthew reports merely that Jesus simply *did not* do many miracles in his hometown (Matt. 13:58).

For some scholars, including all legendary-Jesus theorists, the presence of these biases significantly undermines the historical reliability of these sources. For example, Jesus Seminar founder, Robert Funk, argues that the Gospels are largely fiction partly on the grounds that "the writers are emotionally involved: they believe fervently in the story they are telling, which means they are not impartial observers."[16] So too, some scholars argue that the Gospel authors not only *spun* material for theological purposes, they *created* it for theological purposes.[17] In other words, their theological bias is such that they each tend to make Jesus after their own image, in accordance with particular needs of their faith communities.

The question we must now address is, Does the fact that the Gospel authors are biased warrant such skeptical conclusions? For the following four reasons, we think not.

1. If we were to follow Funk's argument through to its logical conclusion, we'd have to dismiss as unreliable *all* historical reports given by

people who were emotionally involved, who believed fervently in the story they were telling, and who were not impartial. But this seems clearly unreasonable.

To illustrate, would it have been reasonable for leaders of the Western world in 1942 to reject eyewitness reports about what was transpiring in Nazi concentration camps on the grounds that the reporters were emotionally involved with and believed fervently in the things they reported? Clearly not. If what these people were saying was true, as it turned out to be, should we not have *expected* them to be emotionally involved with and to fervently believe in their own reports? Indeed, wouldn't we have been justified in questioning the reliability of these reports if the reporters were *not* emotionally involved with and *did not* fervently believe in what they reported?

So too, if what the Gospel authors say about Jesus is at all close to being accurate, should we not *expect* them to be emotionally involved with and to believe fervently in their own reports? These authors in essence report that Jesus made worldview-jarring claims, lived an outrageously loving life, performed incredible miracles, and rose from the dead. This, they declare, is what convinced them, against their most basic Jewish assumptions, that this crucified man was the long-awaited Messiah—was in fact the embodiment of Yahweh on earth. If these claims are at all accurate, how can we possibly fault them for fervently believing them and for being emotionally involved with them? Indeed, far from dismissing these reports on the grounds that the reporters fervently believe in and are emotionally involved with what they report, it seems to us that the challenge is to explain the fervency and passion without accepting the historical veracity of the reports.

2. If we applied Funk's argument against the reliability of the Gospels consistently, we'd have to reject a great deal of ancient history, because much ancient history was remembered by individuals or groups *precisely because* it meant something to them and they believed fervently in the story they were telling. Indeed, the very idea of doing history from a detached, impartial perspective is a rather modern concept—and, we submit, something of a modern myth. This leads us to our second argument.

If there's anything that has become clear in our postmodern world, it's that *everybody* experiences the world, thinks about the world, and communicates about the world from a biased perspective. Try as we might, *there is no unbiased reporting*. Yet we don't customarily dismiss reports as unreliable for this reason. Yes, biases *color* the truth, but they don't necessarily *undermine* the truth. So, unless one is willing to conclude that humans can *never* reliably report events because of their inevitable biases, it's hardly fair to dismiss the reliability of the Gospels because of their particular biases.

3. As we've seen is the case with so much contemporary critical New Testament scholarship, redaction criticism has to date not adequately appreciated how works written with an oral register differ from works written with a literary register (see chapter 6). Many of the skeptical conclusions redaction critics have come to regarding the Gospels are due to this anachronistic approach.

To illustrate, consider an argument put forth by noted New Testament scholar Werner Kelber.[18] Kelber notices that Mark often presents Peter in a rather negative light. He argues that this reveals that one of Mark's fundamental redactional purposes was to subtly critique the theology of the Jewish-Christian community in Jerusalem, which was under Peter's leadership.[19]

This argument might be plausible if Mark was a modern author who composed his work with a literary register—that is, with the assumption that his work would be privately studied by well-versed, literate individuals. In that case Mark could perhaps have assumed that his intended audience would have been sophisticated enough to pick up subtle, polemical patterns and interpret them in the way Kelber imagines. But, in point of fact, Mark composed his work as an oral recitation of an established oral tradition and thus intended it to be heard in a community context, probably in a single setting.[20]

In this light it seems implausible to suppose that Mark had a deeper, nonhistorical, polemical motive for portraying Peter in a negative light. When Mark's audience heard of Peter's persistent obstinacy throughout this recitation, they would have simply concluded that, as a matter of fact, Peter was a rather obstinate fellow prior to his postresurrection experience.

Our point is that it is anachronistic to read too much theological or polemical motivation into the different ways Gospel authors present their material. Given the oral register of these texts, we should rather consider these differences as simply reflecting the way a particular version of the oral tradition about Jesus evolved in a particular community and the way the material presented itself to the tradent at the time of his composition.[21] It is certainly the case that redaction criticism may disclose certain tendencies within a particular inscribed performance (e.g., a written Gospel) and even within the wider pool of (oral and written) tradition that it serves to express—the previously mentioned tendency of the tradition Matthew expressed to soften potentially embarrassing or offensive material being a case in point. But this is very different from suggesting that the individual author of this Gospel *intentionally edited* his material—let alone that he or any other Gospel author *intentionally fabricated* material—for theological or polemical purposes in a manner reflective of modern (post-Gutenberg), individualistic authors.[22]

4. Our final point also relates to the tendency of modern critics to treat the Gospels anachronistically. As was mentioned in the previous chapter, people writing and reading works within the modern literary paradigm tend to put a premium on originality and novelty. Hence, modern authors are typically praised for "the unique ways in which they produce original creations or for their additions to and novel reshaping of inherited material."[23] This is far removed from the mind-set of authors writing within an ancient oral paradigm. In orally dominant cultures, the goal of performing the community's traditions, whether written or oral, is not primarily originality but rather the activation and faithful retelling of well-known narratives that shape the community's very identity. As we've seen, the community itself typically assumes some of the responsibility to ensure this happens by correcting the tradent in the midst of performance if traditional material is altered in a way that would threaten the essential content.

In this light, the model of the Gospel authors as primarily creative theologians, substantially redacting traditional material and even fabricating material to envision a new Jesus, becomes altogether implausible. Given what we now know about orally dominant cultures, we have no reason to think it would have ever occurred to a Gospel author to strive for the sort of originality many redaction critics seem to imagine.

So we once again conclude that, while each of the Gospel authors was certainly biased, as were the communities whose traditions they expressed, there is good reason to conclude that—as any faithful tradent working with historical tradition that is central to the identity of his or her orally dominant community—they were able to reliably transmit the essential elements of the historical traditions about Jesus.

8

Superfluous and Self-Incriminating Testimony

The Questions of Incidental and Self-Damaging Details

Thus far we have argued that the Gospels pass the first four tests historians customarily submit ancient documents to as they attempt to determine their historical reliability. If ever we have reason to conclude that the copies of an ancient work we possess are reasonably close to the original, we have this with the Gospels. They are works written with a historical intent. The authors were arguably in a position to write reliable history, even if we reject the uniform early attestation of the traditional authorship of these works. And, while they are clearly biased, this ought not necessarily lead to a negative estimation of their historical veracity. We turn, then, to the fifth and sixth questions historians customarily ask concerning ancient documents.[1]

Question 5: Does the document include incidental details or casual information?

All other things being equal, the inclusion of nonideologically motivated incidental or casual information in a document tends to bolster a historian's confidence in its general historical reliability. Of course, if one is dealing with a work that gives evidence of being intentionally fictional, the presence of detail in a narrative is likely to represent nothing more than artistic embellishment. What is interesting about the Gospels, however, is that they do include incidental detail while giving us every reason to believe they were intended to pass on historically rooted tradition of actual events of the past. Not only this, but some of this detail has been independently confirmed as reflecting the situation of first-century Palestine—a point that can bolster our estimation of the reliability of these works.[2]

Treating the Gospels like Any Other Documents

Frequently, scholars outside the field of New Testament studies have appreciated the significance of the incidental detail found in the Gospels more than scholars within the field. For example, Wolfgang Schadewaldt, a respected classical philologist and Homeric scholar who has focused upon issues of authenticity in his own field, assesses the Synoptic Gospels (Matthew, Mark, and Luke) as follows: "As a philologist, someone who has acquired some knowledge of 'literature,' I am particularly concerned here to note that when we read the Synoptic Gospels, we cannot be other than captivated by the experiential vividness with which we are confronted. . . . I know of no other area of history-writing, biography or poetry where I encounter so great a wealth of material in such a small space."[3] If we trust the sensibilities of this esteemed classicist, it seems that if ever we ought to be impressed with the incidental details of an ancient work, we should be so impressed with the Gospels.

A number of other classicists have been similarly impressed with the level of detail and "historical feel" of the Gospels, causing some to wonder how it is that so many New Testament critics arrive at intensely skeptical conclusions about these works. For example, Paul Merkley has wondered how a reputable scholar like Eric Auerbach could disagree so thoroughly with a New Testament critic, Rudolf Bultmann, over the issue of historical intention on the part of the Gospel authors.

> What does it mean that Rudolf Bultmann and Eric Auerbach have before them the same texts, and are impelled by the same passion for truth—and that one can announce with scholarly sobriety that [the Gospel writers] are utterly without interest in historical detail; and the other, on the same sober tone, that the detail of place, setting, characterization and so on is so massive and so obtrusive that we must concede that we are at the source of all the realistic literature of our civilization?[4]

Related to this, psychological studies have shown that "externally gener-ated memories" (i.e., memories produced by actual personal experiences of events within the physical world) have certain characteristics that tend to distinguish them from "internally generated memories" (i.e., memories generated by one's imagination, etc.).[5] Among other things, memories gen-erated by actual external experiences are characterized by more "spatial and temporal" attributes, more "sensory attributes," and "more information or more specific information" than imagination-generated memories.[6] In light of these studies, the previously noted observation of Schadewaldt—"when we read the Synoptic Gospels, we cannot be other than captivated by the experiential vividness with which we are confronted. . . . I know of no other area of history-writing, biography or poetry where I encounter so great a wealth of material in such a small space"[7]—would seem potentially to have important implications for the question of the historical grounding of the Jesus tradition found in the Gospels.

The Presence of Aramaisms

Another class of detail that arguably lends support to the historical veracity of the Gospels concerns the presence of a number of words and expressions that betray an Aramaic origin.[8] For example, when Jesus says that the Pharisees "strain out a gnat but swallow a camel" (Matt. 23:24), it seems most likely that he was making a play on words in the Aramaic language, for the Aramaic words for "gnat" (*galma*) and "camel" (*gamla*) are phonetically quite similar. These Aramaisms are significant because Aramaic was the common language of Palestinian Jews in the first century. Hence, the presence of Aramaisms arguably anchors the Gospel material about Jesus in the first century and on Palestinian soil, thus providing support for the view that this material goes back to Jesus himself.

At the same time, we don't want to make too much of these Aramaisms, for it is frankly impossible to demonstrate whether any particular Aramaism in a Gospel account originated with Jesus himself or rather with one of his early Palestinian followers. Even Joachim Jeremias, one of the prime champions of this criterion, recognized that the mere presence of an Aramaism could not prove the authenticity of any given unit of the Jesus tradition.[9] Nonetheless, when we evaluate the broad pattern of Aramaisms in the Gospels alongside all the other indications of the historical reliability of the oral traditions they express, the Aramaisms can't help but lend weight to the conclusion that we're dealing with material that goes back to Palestinian eyewitnesses.[10]

The Inclusion of Personal Names

One particularly significant class of detail we find in the Gospels is the inclusion of personal names. We've previously discussed the significance of the fact that the Gospels weave their story around named public figures (chapter 3). But just as significant is the inclusion of personal names within the Jesus movement itself.

Richard Bauckham has provided a detailed assessment of this phenomenon and has made a rather compelling case that the presence of these names lends strong support to the historical veracity of these reports.[11] Concentrating on the Synoptic Gospels, Bauckham demonstrates that, while later extracanonical Gospels invent names for characters who are anonymous in the synoptic tradition, the synoptic tradition itself *works in the opposite direction* (assuming the two-source theory, in which Matthew and Luke are believed to have used Mark). Among the Synoptic Gospels there is "an unambiguous tendency toward the elimination of names." Indeed, "in no case does a character unnamed in Mark gain a name in Matthew or Luke."[12]

More specifically, Matthew and Luke both retain Mark's use of a name in four cases (i.e., Simon of Cyrene, Joseph of Arimathea, Mary Magdalene, and Mary the mother of James and Joses). In one case Luke retains a name while Matthew changes it (from Matthew to Levi). In one case Luke retains a name while Matthew drops it (Jairus). And in four cases Matthew and Luke drop the name found in Mark (Bartimaeus, Alexander, Rufus, and Salome).[13] Given this tendency toward eliminating names, and given that many of the Gospel characters appear anonymous from the beginning, Bauckham argues that we have very good grounds for concluding that "these names in the Gospel narratives belong to the original form of the tradition."[14]

More specifically, and most significantly, Bauckham argues that the presence of names in the synoptic tradition can in most cases be best explained by supposing that these characters were specifically remembered because they were eyewitnesses of the traditions to which their names were attached. As such, they would have likely been designated as the authoritative tradents of this tradition and thus would have continued to testify to these traditions throughout their lifetimes.

For example, Bauckham argues that the naming of Cleopas in Luke 24:18 is best explained by assuming that the information contained in this passage derives from Cleopas. The narrative itself does not require a name, and in fact his companion in the account remains anonymous. What explains this? Given the rarity of this name, Bauckham argues that Cleopas should be identified with the Clopas whose wife, Mary, was at the empty tomb (John 19:25). Moreover, according to an early church author named Hegesippus (referred to by Eusebius),[15] Clopas was the brother of Jesus's earthly father, Joseph. As a relative of Jesus and a link to a witness of the empty tomb, Clopas would have been a respected tradent in the early Christian communities. This would easily explain why his name was retained in the tradition. Bauckham persuasively outlines a number of similar cases for considering named characters as eyewitness tradents, including the women at the cross and tomb, Simon of Cyrene and his sons, and certain named recipients of Jesus's healings (e.g., Jairus, Bartimaeus, and Lazarus).

This would also explain why certain names were dropped from the tradition over time. Once an eyewitness tradent was deceased, or if a living tradent was not known to a particular community, there would be no reason to retain his or her name in the oral tradition. Thus, for example, Mark mentions by name not only Simon of Cyrene but also his two sons, Alexander and Rufus (Mark 15:21). Both Matthew and Luke, however, retain Simon's name but, curiously enough, drop the names of his sons (Matt. 27:32; Luke 23:26). Bauckham argues that, given that Mark does not overly use names, the mere fact that Mark expected his audience to know Simon's sons doesn't in and of itself adequately explain the inclusion of their names in his account.[16] What explains the inclusion of these names is rather that "Mark is appealing to Simon's eyewitness testimony, known in the early Christian movement not from his own firsthand account but from that of his sons."[17] After the sons died, or in communities that were unacquainted with these sons, there would no longer be any purpose for including their names.

If Bauckham is on the right track, not only are we afforded a new appreciation of the way in which concrete details in the synoptic tradition constitute evidence of historical remembrance, but the details themselves may well identify eyewitness tradents who were known to testify to the circulating accounts attached to their names. In light of considerations such as these, we conclude that the level of detail and the sort of detail we find in the Gospels is another indication of their general historical trustworthiness.

Question 6: Does the document include self-damaging details?

If the presence of incidental details generally strengthens a historian's estimation of an ancient document, the presence of self-damaging details does so even more. Among other things, self-damaging details suggest that the author was willing to risk damaging his own cause for the sake of remaining faithful to history. In historical-critical Gospel research this phenomenon has been used to test whether the material in the Jesus tradition is authentic—a test known as the "'criterion of embarrassment."[18]

The reasoning behind the application of this criterion in New Testament studies is that early Christians would not have invented material that was counterproductive to their cause—material that put Jesus or themselves in a negative light, made them vulnerable to critiques from opponents, and so forth. On the contrary, one might be inclined to think the tradition would, over time, have tended to minimize or extract altogether aspects of the tradition that were problematic.

So, how do the Gospels fare on the question of the inclusion of self-damaging material? Three points may be made.

Softening of Problematic Material within the Synoptic Tradition

First, a plausible case can be made that some of the potentially embarrassing traditions that came to be expressed in the Gospels underwent a certain amount of softening in the process of their oral transmission. While there were strong community constraints against an oral performer altering the substance of a tradition, as we have seen, this would not prevent an oral tradition from gradually evolving in relatively minor ways, and the softening of potentially embarrassing material is one of the ways we might expect oral traditions to evolve.

The instance of Matthew apparently softening Mark's account of Jesus's inability to perform many miracles in his hometown (see chapter 7) is a likely case in point. An even more informative example might be the way in which Matthew, Luke, and John seem to soften the potentially embarrassing question of why, in Mark's account, Jesus was baptized by John the Baptist (Mark 1:4–11). John's baptism was explicitly said to be for the repentance of sins, so Jesus's baptism could be interpreted as an admission that Jesus was a sinner! Not only this, but the very fact that John baptized Jesus, while Jesus is never said to have baptized John, could give the impression that John was superior to Jesus. Given this, we are not surprised to find Matthew, Luke, and John softening this account in various ways to moderate its potentially embarrassing features (see Matt. 3:13–17; Luke 3:19–22; John 1:29–34).[19]

What is remarkable is not that softening of this sort took place. What is remarkable, rather, is that Mark recounts the potentially embarrassing episode of Jesus's baptism in the first place. What is also noteworthy is that, though they arguably soften Mark's account, Matthew and Luke did not feel free to simply drop it altogether. This strongly suggests that the Gospels' account of Jesus's baptism is rooted in history, for there's no plausible way of explaining how it entered the early Jesus tradition if it is not.

A Wealth of Self-Damaging Material

Our second point is that the potentially embarrassing account of Jesus's baptism by John is hardly an isolated instance in the Gospels. To the contrary, the Gospels are full of embarrassing material we not only can't imagine early Christians inventing but which we might have expected the earliest tradents to drop—*were they not so invested in retaining accurate historical remembrances.* As we should expect, assuming it is the earliest Gospel, Mark tends to present these episodes in their starkest light. Among the potentially embarrassing things we find in this Gospel are the following:

- Jesus's own family did not believe him and even questioned his sanity (3:21; cf. John 7:5).
- Jesus was rejected by people in his hometown and couldn't perform many miracles there (6:2–5).
- Some thought Jesus was in collusion with, and even possessed by, the devil (3:22, 30).
- At times Jesus seemed to rely on common medicinal techniques (7:33; 8:23).
- Jesus's healings weren't always instantaneous (8:22–25).
- Jesus's disciples weren't always able to exorcise demons (9:18), and Jesus's own exorcisms weren't always instantaneous (5:8–13).
- Jesus seemed to suggest he wasn't "good" (10:18).
- Jesus associated with people of ill-repute and gained a reputation of being a glutton and drunkard (2:15–16; cf. Matt. 11:19).
- Jesus sometimes seems to act rudely to people (7:26–27).
- Jesus seemed to disregard Jewish laws, customs, and cleanliness codes (e.g., 2:23–24).
- Jesus often spoke and acted in culturally "shameful" ways (e.g., 3:31–35).
- Jesus cursed a fig tree for not having any figs when he was hungry, despite the fact that it wasn't the season for figs (11:12–14).
- The disciples who were to form the foundation of the new community consistently seem dull, obstinate, and cowardly (e.g., 8:32–33; 10:35–37; 14:37–40, 50).
- Jesus was betrayed by an inner-circle disciple (14:43–46), and Peter cowardly denied any association with him (14:66–72).
- Women were the first to discover Jesus's tomb was empty—while the men were hiding in fear! (16:1–8).

On top of all this, and most significantly, we must remember that the Gospel of Mark, and each subsequent Gospel, is centered on the fact that Jesus was crucified by the Romans. It is hard to imagine a surer way to convince first-century Jews that someone is *not* the Messiah than by telling them that the would-be savior was executed by Israel's military oppressors! To go further and tell them that this would-be savior died a cursed death on a cross would make the sales pitch all the worse (see Deut. 21:22–23). If ever there was something an early, predominantly Jewish, oral tradition would not invent—indeed, if ever there was something we might expect an early, predominately Jewish, oral tradition to smooth over if not conveniently forget altogether—*it is this!* Yet we find that not only do the Gospels retain this event, *it forms the center of their story!*

When we consider these self-damaging features of the Jesus tradition together, it becomes difficult to deny that this tradition is substantially rooted in history. Likewise, it becomes difficult to deny that the Gospel authors were concerned to faithfully convey the essential elements of the Jesus tradition that formed the very self-identity of their respective communities.

The Omission of Relevant Issues

Third, while Mark and the other Gospels include material one might have thought they'd omit, they also omit material one might have thought they would have included if they (and the oral traditions they drew from and fed back into) were more interested in presenting a Jesus who was relevant to the ongoing needs of the community than they were in re-membering Jesus as he actually was. From Paul and other early sources (e.g., Acts, the *Didache*, Clement of Rome), we learn a great deal about the sorts of issues the early church struggled with. *But most of these issues are not addressed in the Gospels.*

For example, we find in the Gospels nothing about how Gentiles were to be integrated into the originally Jewish Jesus movement. Nor do we find anything about how glossolalia and other spiritual gifts were to be used, what food and drink could and couldn't be consumed, what role women could have in the church, or a multitude of other issues we know the early church had to wrestle with. Had the earliest Jesus traditions been inclined to invent a Jesus relevant to their particular concerns rather than simply remember him as he was, *these are precisely the sorts of issues we would have expected the Jesus of the Gospels to address.*[20] The fact that the Gospel traditions retain embarrassing material while failing to insert helpful material testifies to their significant historical interest and thus their general reliability.

9

How Am I Supposed to Believe *That*?

The Questions of Consistency and Plausibility

W e come now to the seventh and eighth tests historians customarily subject ancient documents to as they seek to discern their historical reliability.[1]

Question 7: Is the document internally consistent?

Generally speaking, fabricated accounts tend to include more inconsistencies than truthful accounts. Hence, the absence of inner contradictions contributes to a positive estimation of the document's historical veracity. In the case of the four Gospels, we must ask this question not only in relation to each Gospel, but of the Gospels' relationships with one another, for they each purport to tell essentially the same story.

Space considerations prevent us from investigating in any detail the particular alleged conflicts within and between the Gospels. This has already been carried out by a number of very capable scholars.[2] Rather, what we shall do is make several broad observations, arising mostly out of recent orality studies that we believe put the alleged contradictions within and between the Gospels in a different light. Our argument shall be that when we cease treating these works as though they were written with a modern, literary register and, instead, appreciate them as (written) recitations of an oral tradition intended to be *heard* in a community setting—not *silently studied* in an isolated setting—the level of variation we find within and between the Gospels is not such that it should lessen our confidence in their historical veracity. To the contrary, this level of variation, and even apparent discrepancy, is precisely what we should expect given that these works were written as inscribed recitations of an already well-known oral tradition.

The Discrepancies within and between the Gospels

No informed person denies that there are apparent contradictions within and between the four Gospels. These apparent conflicts can be grouped into four general categories:

1. *Instances of apparently mutually exclusive reports.* For example, did Jesus tell his disciples to take a staff and sandals, as Mark reports (Mark 6:8–9), or *not* to take them, as Matthew reports (Matt. 10:9–10)?
2. *Instances within a Gospel where it appears that one historical event has been recorded as two separate events (called "doublets").* Perhaps the most famous example of this is the two differing accounts of Jesus supernaturally feeding the multitudes (e.g., Mark 6:33–44 and 8:1–9). Many critical scholars argue these two stories are actually two varying accounts of the same story.
3. *Unexplainable omissions or additions within parallel passages.* For example, Mark and Luke record Jesus giving an unqualified prohibition against divorce (Mark 10:11–12; Luke 16:18) while Matthew adds an exception clause (Matt. 5:32; 19:9).
4. *Chronological conflicts.* For example, the episode of Jesus cursing the fig tree and teaching his disciples its lesson occurs over two days in Mark (Mark 11:12–14, 20–25), while Matthew collapses this into one instantaneous event (Matt. 21:18–22).

The question is, do conflicts such as these constitute contradictions that should undermine our assessment of the historical veracity of these works, or can most of these apparent contradictions be harmonized? Again, while we will not here attempt any detailed harmonizations, we offer five broad considerations that we believe render an affirmative answer to the harmonization question much more likely than not.

A Change in Attitude

First, it's important to note that none of these apparent conflicts have been discovered recently. To the contrary, Christian thinkers have known about them since the second century and have offered a variety of plausible ways of resolving them.[3] Clearly, therefore, the insistence on the part of many contemporary New Testament critics, including all legendary-Jesus theorists, that these conflicts are irresolvable and thus undermine the historical trustworthiness of the Gospels is not rooted in any newly discovered facts. Nor is it rooted in any new evidence demonstrating that the proposed ways of harmonizing these conflicts are all implausible. Rather, this insistence is rooted in a relatively new attitude many modern scholars *bring to* the data.

More specifically, proposed ways of reconciling conflicts within and between the Gospels have become implausible to many contemporary scholars, not necessarily because they are inherently so, but because the naturalistic worldview that has been embraced by these modern scholars renders them so. That is, because the Gospels contain miracles, which the naturalistic worldview disallows, these scholars bring to these works a skeptical attitude that renders attempts to resolve their apparent contradictions superfluous.

To come at this from a slightly different direction, one attempts to resolve contradictions within and between documents only if he or she believes it's at least *possible* the works in question are generally trustworthy. If, instead, one has *already concluded* that a set of documents are *not* generally trustworthy, then the appearance of contradictions simply confirms what one assumes he or she already knew: namely, that the documents in question are not reliable. Indeed, in the case of the Gospels, many critics assume that attempts to reconcile apparent conflicts are always theologically motivated (namely, trying to defend a conception of biblical inspiration) and thus cannot be judged as representing good, historical-critical scholarship.

The prejudicial nature of this skeptical stance is shown in the fact that, from a strictly historiographical perspective, the level of apparent conflicts between the Gospels *is relatively normal*. Rarely in history do we find multiple witnesses to an event that do not contain apparent contradictions. As Gilbert Garraghan explains in his *Guide to Historical Method*, "Almost any critical history that discusses the evidence for important statements will furnish examples of discrepant or contradictory accounts and the attempts which are made to reconcile them."[4] Recently, the necessity of engaging in harmonization attempts was recognized by film writer and director James Cameron while working on the script for his blockbuster movie *The Titanic*. In a documentary interview on the making of his film, Cameron explained that he discovered numerous conflicts in the available eyewitness reports about what happened on the Titanic's fateful voyage. Some of these reports were given in court under oath, and there was absolutely no reason to doubt their essential veracity. Yet, as is typical of multiple eyewitness accounts, these reports contained a variety of apparent discrepancies. Despite these apparent conflicts, however, Cameron reported that he found enough in common among the reports to start reconstructing the main lines of what actually happened.[5]

From discrepant reports of Alexander the Great by Arrian and Plutarch to the differing accounts of Hannibal crossing the Alps by Livy and Polybius all the way up to conflicts between reports found every week in our various news magazines, *discrepancies are the norm*—which means attempts at harmonization accounts *must be the rule* as we try to discern what actually happened. Because of this, the standard historiographical assumption is that conflicting data that is purportedly historical deserves to be read as sympathetically as possible, with attempts to harmonize the conflicting data carried out before one dismisses the data as unreliable on the basis of these apparent conflicts. The only apparent reason legendary-Jesus theorists don't extend this same courtesy to the Gospels is because they have already decided—for metaphysical, not historiographical, reasons (see chapter 1)—that the Gospels aren't trustworthy. And this, we contend, is prejudicial.   .

The Fragmentary Nature of Oral Recitations

Second, if searching for ways of harmonizing apparently conflicting accounts is generally warranted when trying to discern what actually happened, it is all the more so when one is dealing with apparent conflicts between texts written in an orally dominant context, such as the Gospels. As was mentioned in chapter 5, recent orality studies have demonstrated that orally oriented sources, whether written or oral, presuppose a much broader tradition that is typically well-known to the listening audience. This broader tradition forms what can be called the "mental text" of the community, and it forms the assumed context within which all shared episodes of the oral tradition, whether written or orally performed, make sense.

For this reason, orally oriented tradition employs a good deal of "metonymy," which is "a mode of signification wherein a part stands for the whole."[6] Hence, most of what is intended to be communicated by tradents within the community is *not explicitly stated* in any given oral or written performance. They typically record "the relevant facts very partially . . . relying on a background of memory and witnesses."[7] And in light of these considerations, we must conclude we will always misunderstand works written with an oral register if we treat them as if they were modern, autonomous, self-sufficient works.

Rosalind Thomas makes this point well when she notes that ancient documents "presuppose knowledge which is simply remembered and not written down." Far from being autonomous works, as texts with literate registers tend to be, ancient works "cannot perform their task without backing from non-written communication." Hence, she concludes, "It becomes difficult to separate oral and written modes in any meaningful sense except in the most basic one (i.e., what was written down and what was not). *It is surely only our modern confidence in and obsession with the written text which see documents as entirely self-sufficient.*"[8]

The implications of these observations are significant when it comes to assessing the apparent conflicts within and between the Gospels. It means that to treat these works responsibly we *have* to try to imagine the broader tradition the audience and author shared and within which the individual, fragmentary, elliptical accounts were originally understood. And this means we have to try to imagine a broader oral context within which the apparent conflicts between accounts can be harmonized. In this light, we must conclude that the refusal of skeptical scholars to acknowledge the legitimacy of attempting to harmonize the Gospel accounts is not only prejudicial; it is *fundamentally opposed to the very nature of the Gospel texts themselves.*

These observations, of course, don't imply that we can simply assume that if we had access to the broader oral tradition of the early Christians, all apparent conflicts would be instantly resolved. From a strictly histo-riographical perspective, we have to concede that it's possible that various traditions gradually modified their contents in the course of transmission in ways that simply contradict other traditions, even by ancient oral stan-dards. But it does imply that modern scholars shouldn't assume that what appears to us to be a contradiction would *not* be reconciled if we had access to the broader oral traditions the written Gospels drew on and fed back into. And, therefore, it implies we shouldn't dismiss plausible proposals as to how apparent conflicts might be harmonized in light of the broader, presupposed oral tradition shared by the Gospels' original audience. To the contrary, as we've said, to read the Gospels nonanachronistically, we *have* to try to imagine this broader shared background.

On Remembering Things, Not Words

Third, orality studies have consistently demonstrated that the focus of memory in oral traditions is generally on *"things,"* not *"words."*[9] As we've said, oral performers are typically given significant leeway in how they retell a story, so long as they convey the essence of the story accurately. This means that we can expect to find the essential *voice* of Jesus in the early church's oral tradition, but we cannot suppose early Christians would, as a rule, have been invested in preserving the *exact words* of Jesus. It also suggests that we are likely missing the mark if we suppose there to be any genuine conflict between the different ways the Gospels record the teachings and events of Jesus's life. Modern, literate-minded people might find a contradiction between one Gospel author recording Jesus telling his disciples to wear sandals (Mark 6:9) while the others have him forbidding them (Matt. 10:10; Luke 10:4), but it's very unlikely an ancient person would have been con-cerned in the least with such a variance in detail. For the essential point of Jesus's teaching is the same in all three accounts—namely, the disciples were to trust God for their provisions while doing missionary work.[10]

Schematic Wholes over Discrete Facts

Fourth, and closely related to this, we now know that oral traditions typically place far more emphasis on schematic wholes than on isolated details.[11] As we saw in chapter 5, Bultmann and most other early form critics assumed that oral traditions could only pass on small units of tradition, not extended narratives. But, as we've already shown, *they had it exactly wrong*. Generally speaking, explicit and implicit extended narratives and integrated schematic complexes are precisely the sorts of things that are viewed as essential to oral traditions. What is not so essential is *the precise way* events are ordered and remembered in any given oral performance.

S. A. Sowayan's insightful study of Arabic historical narrative in the oral mode is instructive at this point. Sowayan demonstrated that orally transmitted narratives are designed as *suwalif*—meaning, literally, "to have happened in the past." In sharp contrast to the widespread assumption of many Western scholars that oral traditions tend to lack genuine historical interest, Sowayan has shown that the traditional narratives he studied were centered on "historical events and biographical or social circumstances connected with the immediate, or remote, past."[12] Yet, he has also demonstrated that the order in which events are presented in any given oral performance has more to do with the process of remembering on the part of the performer than it does with the order in which events actually took place. "As one remembers," he says, "one narrates. . . . Once the narrative begins, it can be developed in any of several possible directions, depending upon the performance context."[13]

Sowayan fleshes out the nature of these historical, oral recitations when he continues:

> A long narrative is a cluster of smaller narratives which are imbedded and interlinked with each other. The swarming of the various narratives to the narrator's mind as he starts, and the disentanglement of the various episodes as they come in the way of one another and crowd in his breast . . . can be likened to the flocking of thirsty camels to the drinking-trough. . . . At times, stories come in the way of one another and the narrator may find himself compelled to suspend an ongoing story in the middle to tell a different one. . . . This is because narratives are plentiful and interconnected.[14]

Numerous orality studies have found a similar pattern in a wide variety of cultural settings.[15] Unless they are familiar with it, this sort of nonlinear, creative flexibility in how material is presented may strike modern, highly literate people as involving historical inaccuracies and contradictions.

But, as a matter of fact, such a conclusion would merely evidence how thoroughly these post-Gutenberg folk had misunderstood the nature of communicative performances within orally dominant cultures.

It is no accident that the Gospels each exhibit this interesting balance between essential fixity and creative flexibility. As tradents operating within the communicative content of an oral register, the Gospel authors freely rearrange events and sayings. They sometimes seem to collate or divide up events (as we previously noted Matthew doing with Mark's version of the cursing of the fig tree). At times they seem to intentionally do this for topical reasons. But, for all we know, at other times they may do so simply because this is how the material presented itself to them as they were composing their works. In any event, *by the standards of orally dominant cultures*, the fact that the way events and sayings are ordered is markedly different in each Gospel does not constitute a contradiction and does not in the least compromise the genuineness of the historical interest or capabilities of the Gospel authors. To think otherwise, as many legendary-Jesus theorists do, is to think anachronistically.

Jesus as an Itinerant Preacher

A fifth and final implication of orality studies for our understanding of apparent conflicts within and between the Gospels centers on the itinerant ministry of Jesus himself. Because the modern critical study of the Gospels has been driven by a literary paradigm, insufficient attention has been paid to the realities and constraints that would have characterized Jesus's itinerant ministry within an orally dominant culture.[16] Only recently have a few modern scholars begun to seriously work through the implications of the fact that Jesus's ministry would have, of necessity, been characterized by multiple oral performances of the same—or at least very similar—material.

Werner Kelber hits the mark when he notes that "reiteration and variation of words and stories must be assumed for Jesus' own proclamation. Multiple, variable renditions, while observable in tradition, are highly plausible in Jesus' own oral performance."[17] N. T. Wright notes the "enormous implications . . . this [observation] has for synoptic criticism" when he argues that "within the peasant oral culture of his day, Jesus must have left behind him, not one or two isolated traditions, but a veritable mare's nest of anecdotes, and also of sentences, aphorisms, rhythmic sayings, memorable stories with local variations, [etc.]."[18]

This implies that, in all likelihood, many of the variations of Jesus's teachings found in the Gospels—variations that modern, literate-minded scholars tend to explain by appealing to the different redactional purposes of each individual author—are probably better explained simply as oral variations performed by Jesus himself.[19] This also may explain certain doublets found in the Gospels. An itinerant preacher like Jesus would have said and done very similar things in different locations at different times. To reject such an explanation, as many skeptical scholars do, is to "simply have no historical imagination for what an itinerant ministry, within a peasant culture, would look like."[20]

To conclude this section, it is clear that by the standards of a modern, *literary* paradigm, the Gospels indeed contain contradictions. What we have been arguing, however, is that evaluating them by these modern standards is anachronistic. Judged by the conventions and constraints of their own orally dominant cultural context and read sympathetically with an imaginative appreciation for the wider oral tradition they were written to express and feed back into, the Gospels are shown to exhibit the sort of broad internal consistency that suggests that the authors intended to faithfully record the essential aspects of Jesus's life and that they were successful at doing so.

Question 8: Does the document contain inherently implausible events?

To the extent that a document asks us to believe things that seem inherently improbable, historians are inclined to judge them as historically unreliable. Of course, this leaves unanswered the question of how we are to decide what is and is not "inherently improbable."[21]

This question is especially important when it comes to assessing documents, like the Gospels, that contain reports of supernatural occurrences. For, as we have argued (chapter 1), whether a historian finds such accounts to be inherently improbable will largely depend on what presuppositions he or she *brings to* the investigation. Indeed, in the case of the Gospels it seems evident that these presuppositions play a decisive role, for, as we are seeing, the Gospel accounts give us many other reasons to accept that they are, in fact, generally reliable. Certainly the general way these works recount the events of Jesus's life and ministry, including miraculous episodes, is relatively sober and realistic—as evidenced, for example, by the way they include self-damaging material (chapter 8). These works are characteristically devoid of the sort of implausible eulogizing common in legends and frequently found in later legendary gospels. Legendary-Jesus theorists nevertheless find these works to be implausible—largely because they just "know" at the start that supernatural events, such as those reported in the Gospels, cannot possibly be rooted in history.

As we argued in chapter 1, this stance of dogmatic naturalism is nothing more than an ethnocentric metaphysical assumption that has to be accepted on faith. There are no compelling philosophical, logical, or historical arguments that require us to assume (or even justify) this stance. Moreover, this assumption has not been shared by most people throughout history, and it remains unshared by most people today—including the vast majority of people in contemporary Western culture. It is an assumption held by a relatively small group of Western academics who insist that their own culturally conditioned way of looking at the world is the only true way, all the evidence to the contrary notwithstanding.

Though these scholars often hold that their naturalistic assumption is the cornerstone for all truly critical historiography, we submit that, as a matter of fact, it is not nearly critical enough. Rather, a truly critical approach would begin by being critical of the culturally conditioned nature of its own presuppositions—including the academic, Western presupposition that truly supernatural events cannot occur.

If one can genuinely remain open to the possibility that such naturalistic presuppositions are incorrect, we submit that there is widespread evidence throughout the world, and compelling evidence within the Gospels themselves, that these presuppositions are, in fact, incorrect. And once the naturalistic assumption has been suspended, one finds there is nothing in the Gospels that is inherently implausible—at least not to the point that would justify calling the general reliability of these works into question.

10

Jesus and Ancient Non-Christian Writers

The Question of Literary Corroboration

The final two questions customarily asked by historians assessing a document's historical reliability are not about the internal characteristics of the document in question, as were the previous eight. Rather, they are about the extent to which evidence outside of the document confirms or refutes claims made by the document. More specifically, these last two questions address the relation a document has to other *literary* evidence, on the one hand, and *archaeological* evidence, on the other. We shall address the question of literary evidence in this chapter and the question of archaeological evidence in the next.[1]

Question 9: Does literary evidence corroborate the claims made by the document?

To the extent that the historical claims made by a document can be corroborated by other ancient documents that are deemed trustworthy, a historian's confidence in the historical reliability of the document is enhanced, all other things being equal.

It must be said at the outset that there is very little by way of ancient literary evidence that confirms or refutes claims made by the Gospels. This should not surprise us, however. More often than not, claims made by ancient documents can't be corroborated, if for no other reason than that the vast majority of all that was written in the ancient world has perished in the sands of time. Not only this, but historians in the ancient Roman world typically wrote under the authority of governing officials. They thus tended to be interested only in matters that were relevant to the administration they worked for. Since the earliest Jesus movement was a small, sectarian, Jewish group in a rather remote region of the Roman Empire, and since new religious movements were not uncommon in the ancient world, one shouldn't expect to find either Jesus or the movement he birthed referred to by ancient historians.

Nevertheless, while relevant literary evidence is meager, it's not nonexistent (as some legendary-Jesus theorists contend). And the little relevant literary evidence we find arguably helps corroborate certain claims made in the Gospels. The following are the most important pieces of evidence that plausibly support aspects of the early Jesus tradition.

Thallus

The first possible noncanonical reference to an event recorded in the Gospels concerns an obscure historian named Thallus, who wrote a three-volume history in the mid-50s. As with most ancient works, this document has not survived. It is referred to by other writers, however, and the reference that interests us comes from Julius Africanus, a third-century Christian historian. In the course of discussing the prolonged darkness that occurred on the day Jesus died, Julius notes that "in the third book of his history Thallus calls this darkness an eclipse of the sun—wrongly in my opinion."[2] It thus seems that Thallus confirms the Gospels' accounts of the unusual darkness that engulfed the land when Jesus was crucified (Matt. 27:45; Mark 15:33; Luke 23:44).

Some argue that Thallus may have simply been accepting as fact a Christian (legendary) tradition about the supernatural darkness that occurred during Jesus's crucifixion and offering an alternative explanation of it.[3] This isn't impossible, of course, but it strikes us as unlikely. Why would a Roman historian take the claims of a recent and relatively minor religious sect so seriously that it would warrant a counterexplanation, *unless he believed the claim to be true on other grounds?* Indeed, one wonders why a Roman historian would bother to incorporate something as common as an ordinary eclipse into his work unless there was something unusual about this particular eclipse that continued to make it a topic of conversation two decades after it happened.

If the account of the prolonged darkness is rooted in history, we can understand why it might have been widely remembered and why Thallus would feel the need to offer a counterexplanation for it—especially if a despised cult (the Christians) was using this publicly acknowledged event to further their own cause. It thus seems to us more likely than not that Thallus's remark constitutes the earliest external corroboration of an event in the Gospels. And the confirmation is all the more significant because it involves a potentially supernatural occurrence.

Pliny

Around AD 110, while governor of Bithynia, Pliny wrote to the Emperor Trajan asking him for advice on dealing with Christians in his territory. In the course of the letter, Pliny recounts information about Christians he had gathered from people who had defected from the Christian faith under threat of death. He says,

> They [former Christians] assured me that the sum total of their error consisted in the fact that they regularly assembled on a certain day before daybreak. They recited a hymn antiphonally to Christus as if to a god, and bound themselves with an oath not to commit any crime, but to abstain from theft, robbery, adultery, breach of faith, and embezzlement of property entrusted to them. After this it was their custom to separate, and then to come together again to partake of a meal, but of an ordinary and innocent one.[4]

From this letter we learn that, despite Nero's attempt to wipe Christianity out and other persecutions, by the early second century the Jesus movement had spread to Bithynia, and its followers had become so numerous it had to be dealt with by the local governor. We also learn from this letter that both Christians and non-Christians at this time assumed Jesus had existed as a real, historical person and that Christians worshipped him as divine, confirming the view of Jesus given in the New Testament. Thus, even apart from all evidence from Paul or the Gospels, Pliny's testimony challenges us to explain how a movement begun among Jews and on Jewish soil could have come to believe that a man was "a god" and could have experienced the kind of rapid growth it obviously experienced.

Suetonius

In the fifth volume of his *Lives of the Caesars*, the Roman historian Suetonius refers to the expulsion of Jews from Rome during Claudius's reign in AD 49. Writing around AD 120, he notes that Claudius "expelled the Jews from Rome, since they were always making disturbances because of the instigator Chrestus."[5] A rather plausible case can be made for concluding that the "Chrestus" Suetonius speaks of is in fact Christ. Chrestus was a common name among Gentiles but was not used by Jews, so far as we know.[6] At the same time, one can easily understand Suetonius mistaking a Jewish title ("Christ") he was unfamiliar with for a common Greek name and thus emending it to *Chrestus*.[7]

Also significant is the fact that Luke tells us that Jews were temporarily expelled from Rome by Claudius because a riot had broken out over the preaching of Christ (Acts 18:2). Bringing all this together, it's not hard to surmise that Suetonius mistakenly understood a riot that was allegedly instigated by Christians as being instigated by Christ himself, whose name as we've suggested, he mistook to be the proper Greek name *Chrestus*.

Of course the theory is speculative, but not implausibly so. The alternative is to suppose that a Jewish man with an un-Jewish name started a riot that got all the Jews in Rome expelled and that Luke wrongly, and quite coincidentally, attributed this expulsion to a Jewish uprising against Christians. But this strikes us as even more speculative and implausible. If our suggestion is accepted, we not only have here a secular reference to Christ, we have a confirmation of the accuracy of Luke's account in Acts and yet further testimony to how quickly the early Christian movement grew. Less than two decades after its founder died—hence while eyewitnesses (including the founder's brother) were still alive—this movement was large enough to incite a riot that led an emperor to temporarily expel Jews from Rome.

Celsus

In the late second century, the Neoplatonist philosopher Celsus wrote the first known full-scale attack on Christianity, entitled *True Doctrine*.[8] What's significant about this work is that Celsus argues that Jesus was a sorcerer and a magician. We find this charge raised a number of times in later Jewish tradition and, according to the Gospels, it goes back to opponents of Jesus himself (Matt. 12:24; Mark 3:22; Luke 11:15). What's most interesting about this is that no one in the ancient world ever flatly denied that Jesus performed miracles—let alone that he existed. They rather granted that he performed miracles but offered different ways of explaining them (e.g., demonic power, trickery). This uniform agreement is difficult to explain on the assumption that the Jesus story was in fact a recently created legend at the time the Gospels were written. If it was indeed largely legendary, wouldn't at least some of the numerous critics of the early Jesus movement have raised this charge against it?

In this light, we consider Celsus's charge to be confirmation of the existence of Jesus and the apparently miraculous nature of his ministry.

Lucian of Samosata

Sometime around AD 165 Lucian wrote a book entitled *The Death of Peregrinus*, in which he blamed the ruin of Peregrinus on Christians, based on the fact that they discouraged the worship of Peregrinus's traditional gods. At one point Lucian refers to Christ as "that other whom [Christians] still worship, the man who was crucified in Palestine because he introduced this new cult into the world."[9] What's most interesting about this passage is that the word Lucian uses for "crucifixion" (*anaskolopizein*) is not the common one, and it's certainly not the one used in the Gospels (*stauroun*). It literally means "to impale," which is not how any early Christian described Jesus's death.

This deviation from Christian tradition may indicate that Lucian is relying on an independent, non-Christian tradition about Jesus. As Craig Evans points out, it "suggests that Lucian's knowledge of Jesus, 'the man crucified in Palestine,' may not be limited to Christian tradition."[10] Hence, Lucian may provide independent confirmation of Jesus's crucifixion.

Tacitus

More important than all the previous secondary sources is a passage found in Tacitus's *Annals*. Cornelius Tacitus was proconsul of Asia for two years (AD 112–113), and he authored two works that survive today only in portions. The *Annals* was his second work and consisted of sixteen volumes in which he rather meticulously covers Roman history from Augustus through Nero (AD 14–68). The portion of the *Annals* that is of interest to us (15:44) was most likely written around AD 115. The passage comes in the context of a discussion of the great fire of Rome under Nero's reign. Tacitus reports:

> Therefore, to squelch the rumor [that the burning of Rome had taken place by Nero's own order], Nero supplied (as culprits) and punished in the most extraordinary fashion those hated for their vice, whom the crowd called "Christians." Christus, the author of their name, had suffered the death penalty during the reign of Tiberius, by sentence of the procurator Pontius Pilate. The pernicious superstition was checked for a time, only to break out once more, not merely in Judea, the origin of the evil, but in the capital itself, where all things horrible and shameful collect and are practiced.[11]

This passage confirms the Gospels' report that Jesus was executed during the reign of Tiberius (i.e., AD 14–37) and when Pilate was procurator (or prefect, see below; AD 26–36). Tacitus also confirms that within a few decades after it began in Judea, and despite being regarded as a "pernicious superstition" and "hated for vice," this movement had spread with remarkable speed—to the point where, by the early 60s, Nero could plausibly make Christians scapegoats for a citywide fire.[12]

Some legendary-Jesus theorists try to argue that this passage was a Christian interpolation, but their arguments are not particularly strong.[13] There is no textual evidence to support this claim, and, in any case, it's very difficult to imagine why a Christian would insert into Tacitus's work a description of Christianity as a "pernicious superstition" or say that Christians were "hated" for their "vice." Nor would one expect a Christian interpolator to limit the account of Christian origins to Jesus's execution. One would rather have thought the interpolator would at least allude to Jesus's resurrection. We thus find ourselves in agreement with John

Meier when he concludes, "Despite some feeble attempts to show that this text is a Christian interpolation in Tacitus, the passage is obviously genuine."[14]

Others have attempted to argue that Tacitus is simply being unreliable at this point. They point out that Tacitus identifies Pilate as a "procurator" of Judea, though archaeological evidence suggests that the official term used for Pilate's position during his reign was "prefect."[15] "Procurator" was the term used in Tacitus's day and, it is argued, he anachronistically applied it to Pilate.

The argument simply doesn't hold up, however. It is entirely possible that Tacitus was intentionally anachronistic for the sake of clarity since "procurator" was the accepted title of Pilate's position among Tacitus's audience. Even more significantly, archaeological and literary evidence suggests that these and other terms for reigning officials were rather fluid in the first century.

For example, though the "Pilate-stone" discovered at Caesarea Maritima in 1961 gives Pilate the title "prefect," both Philo (*On the Embassy to Gaius* 38) and Josephus (*Jewish War*, 2.169) refer to him as "procurator" (the Greek word is *epitropos*), just as Tacitus does. Indeed, Josephus sometimes uses the two terms interchangeably.[16] Hence, there is no basis for questioning Tacitus's reliability on these grounds. Indeed, it is significant that Tacitus is generally regarded among scholars as being one of the most accurate of all ancient historians.[17]

We thus take it as firmly established that Tacitus provides extrabiblical confirmation of Jesus's crucifixion and, once again, challenges us to explain the origin and rapid growth of this Jewish movement that regarded a recent contemporary as the embodiment of Yahweh while his brother and closest disciples were still alive.

Josephus's James Passage

Arguably even more important than Tacitus's reference to Jesus are two passages found in Josephus's work. The first of these two references may be called "the James passage" since it centers on James, the brother of Jesus. It reads, "When, therefore, Ananus [the high priest] was of this [angry] disposition, he thought he had now a proper opportunity [to exercise his authority]. Festus was now dead, and Albinus was but upon the road. So he assembled the sanhedrin of judges, and brought before them the brother of Jesus, who was called Christ, whose name was James (*Jewish Antiquities* 20.9.1)."[18]

This passage confirms that Jesus existed and, in fact, was known well enough in the late first century that Josephus could assume his audience knew of him. Only on this assumption can we account for Josephus identifying James by referring to him as Christ's brother. Not only this, but Josephus confirms that James was Jesus's biological brother—a point that is particularly significant because Paul knew James as a contemporary, which in turn entails that Paul viewed his brother, Jesus, as a recent contemporary (see chapter 3). Hence, this passage once again forces the question of how this first-century Jew could have arisen to the status of Yahweh embodied while his brother and disciples were still alive—indeed, with his brother becoming one of his followers. This is not at all easy to explain as a legend, especially in a first-century Palestinian Jewish context. It forces us, therefore, to once again seriously consider the possibility that the Jesus of history was indeed someone who had the kind of supernatural power and authority the Gospels ascribe to him.

Some scholars, however, argue that the James passage was inserted into the text by a later Christian copyist. The most prominent reasons given for this conclusion are the following:

- Though Josephus mentions many messiah figures, he never uses the term *Christos*. The use of this term in this passage thus suggests a Christian wrote it.
- The fact that Josephus mentions Jesus before he gives his account of John the Baptist suggests that a Christian wrote it, for a Christian would have wanted Jesus to assume pride of place over John.
- The passage involves a very negative assessment of Ananus the high priest. However, when Josephus mentions Ananus in his earlier work, *Jewish War* (4.5.2), he is quite positive toward him.
- The passage reads naturally without any reference to Jesus. Nothing is lost if Jesus's name is removed. Since the story is about Ananus, not James, there would be no need for Josephus to include an additional qualifier on James. A Christian interpolator, on the other hand, would have motive to add this qualifier.[19]

The case against the James passage initially looks formidable. But on closer examination, its apparent strength diminishes considerably. We offer five considerations.

1. It is worth noting that there is no textual evidence that this passage has been inserted. While certainly not decisive against the interpolation theory given the relative scarcity of ancient manuscripts of *Antiquities*, this consideration nevertheless may cast some initial doubt on the interpolation theory.

2. While it is true that Josephus nowhere else uses the title "Christ" of alleged messiahs, we can easily imagine why he would do so when describing the brother of James. Josephus mentions twenty-one other people with the name Jesus! Indeed, in the very same section as the James passage he mentions a certain "Jesus, the son of Damneus." It seems Josephus simply knew (and expected his audience to know) that the brother of James was "called Christ" by his followers and so distinguished him from the other men named Jesus he'd already mentioned.[20] Not only this, but the very fact that Josephus says he was *"called* Christ" rather than simply referring to "Jesus the Christ" would seem to suggest that we are dealing with a Jewish historian who merely wanted to identify James by specifying his well-known brother—not a Christian interpolator.

3. As Craig Evans notes, there is in this passage "nothing Christian, or positive, in the reference to James or Jesus. The whole point seems to be to explain why Ananus was disposed as High Priest."[21] If a Christian had added this passage, one would have thought that much more would have been made of James and especially Jesus. Instead, as John Meier notes, all we have here is "a passing, almost blasé reference to someone called James."[22] Related to this, early Christians did not refer to James in the matter-of-fact way this passage does—namely, simply calling him "the brother of Jesus." Rather, they typically used more laudable titles such as "the brother of the Lord" or "the brother of the Savior."[23]

4. While it is true that Josephus's view of Ananus in the James passage is more negative than what we find in his early work, *Jewish War*, it's also true that there is an unmistakable negative shift in Josephus's general attitude toward Jewish religious and political leadership between these two works.[24] The negative view of Ananus in this passage is consistent with this general shift. Hence, nothing of any significance can be read into it.

5. Perhaps most significantly, the account of James's martyrdom in Josephus differs markedly from the traditional Christian account. From later Christian sources (namely, Eusebius, Hegesippus, and Clement of Alexandria) we learn that early Christians believed James was first thrown from the battlement of the temple by scribes and Pharisees. They then began to stone him but were stopped by a priest. James was finally clubbed to death by laundrymen. In contradiction to this, Josephus says James was simply stoned to death by order of the high priest Ananus. Moreover, according to the Christian tradition, James was killed just prior to Vespasian's siege of Jerusalem in AD 70. According to Josephus, however, he died before the Jewish war broke out, around AD 62. The fact that the Josephus account differs so dramatically from the traditional Christian narrative suggests that this passage is not a Christian interpolation.[25]

For these reasons we conclude that it is more probable than not that the James passage is authentic. As such, it confirms that Jesus existed, that he was relatively well-known by the late first century, that he had a brother named James, and that they lived just prior to when Ananus was high priest, thus situating Jesus and James in history precisely when the Gospels do.

The Testimonium Flavianum

The last reference to Jesus by a nonbiblical source is also from Josephus and is by far the most famous, perhaps the most important, and certainly the most controversial. It is known as the *Testimonium Flavianum*, which is Latin for "the testimony of Flavius"—Josephus's first name. In the version that has come down to us, we read:

> About this time there lived Jesus, a wise man, if indeed one ought to call him a man. For he was one who wrought surprising feats and was a teacher of such people as accept the truth gladly. He won over many Jews and many of the Greeks. He was the Messiah. When Pilate, upon hearing him accused by men of the highest standing among us, had condemned him to be crucified, those who had in the first place come to love him did not give up their affection for him. On the third day he appeared to them restored to life, for the prophets of God had prophesied these and countless other marvelous things about him. And the tribe of the Christians, so called after him, has still to this day not disappeared (*Jewish Antiquities* 18.3.3).[26]

Here we have the most important Jewish historian in ancient times apparently acknowledging not only that Jesus existed but that he was wise, performed miracles, was the Messiah, was crucified, and even rose from the dead! Unfortunately, almost all scholars agree that the passage is, in whole or in part, a Christian interpolation. The most persuasive consideration is that there are three phrases in this passage that are obviously Christian.

- "*. . . if indeed one ought to call him a man.*" This is clearly an implicit allusion to Christ's deity.
- "*He was the Messiah.*" Not only would no non-Christian affirm this, but it seems that Josephus didn't even believe that the Messiah would be Jewish. Rather, he seems to have thought that his patron, the Roman general Vespasian, was the messiah (e.g., see *Jewish War*, 6.5.4).
- "*On the third day he appeared to them restored to life, for the prophets of God had prophesied these and countless other marvelous things about him.*" This whole sentence is filled with distinctly Christian content. The phrase "on the third day" was a formulaic expression used by early Christians (e.g., Matt. 16:21; 17:23; 20:19; 1 Cor. 15:4). The claim that Jesus was restored to life is obviously a Christian confession of the resurrection. And the claim that Old Testament prophets foretold aspects of Jesus's life was a common early Christian theme.

On top of all this, the *Testimonium* isn't referred to by early Christian apologists such as Irenaeus, Tertullian, and Origen, though it's clear they were familiar with Josephus's *Antiquities*. If Josephus had said the things this passage has him say about Jesus, it's hard to imagine early Christians not seizing it to their advantage. Even more damaging is the fact that Origen twice noted that Josephus did *not* believe Jesus was the Messiah (see *Against Celsus*, 1.45; *Commentary on Matthew*, 10.17). It thus seems close to certain that the passage as it stands is at least partly a Christian interpolation.

In Support of a Reconstructed Version of the Testimonium

On the other hand, there are several compelling arguments that have led many scholars to conclude that this passage isn't *entirely* an interpolation. Once the three obviously Christian phrases are removed, the passage reads like something a first-century Jewish historian could have said about Jesus. If we remove the Christian phrases from the text, we are left with the following:

> About this time there lived Jesus, a wise man. For he was one who wrought surprising feats and was a teacher of such people as accept the truth gladly. He won over many Jews and many of the Greeks. When Pilate, upon hearing him accused by men of the highest standing among us, had condemned him to be crucified, those who had in the first place come to love him did not give up their affection for him. And the tribe of the Christians, so called after him, has still to this day not disappeared.[27]

There are six lines of consideration that, in our opinion, support something like this reconstructed version of the *Testimonium* as what Josephus himself actually wrote:

1. Acknowledging that Jesus was a "wise man" and a doer of "surprising feats" would have been no problem for Josephus. As most New Testament scholars agree, Jesus was widely known as a teacher and a miracle worker in the ancient world, for better or for worse. Josephus is merely noting what would have been commonly known traditions about Jesus of Nazareth in the late first century. In fact, there isn't anything in this passage that a first-century Jewish writer couldn't have said about Jesus.

2. Significantly enough, a tenth-century Arabic translation of the *Testimonium* has been discovered, and it is quite close to the reconstructed passage offered above.[28] The phrase, "if indeed one ought to call him a man," is completely absent. The phrase, "He was the Messiah," is relocated to the end and reads, "He was perhaps the Messiah." And the claim about Jesus's postmortem appearances after the third day is preceded by, "They reported that. . . ."

   A good number of reputable scholars believe this suggests that the author of the Arabic version of the *Testimonium* had access to a version of *Antiquities* whose textual tradition predated the Christian interpolation. Thus, the Arabic text likely helps confirm something like the reconstructed version of the *Testimonium* offered above. Largely on this basis James Charlesworth concludes, "We can now

be as certain as historical research will presently allow that Josephus
did refer to Jesus in *Antiquities* 18.63–64."[29]

3. Not only does this reconstructed passage contain things that a Jewish historian could have said about Jesus, it also contains things
   that a Christian interpolator would most likely *not* have said. The
   statement that Jesus "won over" many Jews *and Gentiles* seems
   inconsistent with a Christian interpolator. For the Christian tradition, as contained in the Gospels, gives no indication that Jesus
   ever emphasized evangelism among the Gentiles—let alone that
   he was successful in doing so. Indeed, the Gospels present Jesus
   as intentionally pursuing a distinctly Jewish following during his
   lifetime (e.g., Matt. 10:5). As Meier notes, it seems much less likely
   that a Christian interpolator would have contradicted the Gospels'
   own picture of Jesus's ministry than that Josephus himself simply
   "retrojected the situation of his own day," wherein many among
   Jesus's followers were Gentile.[30]

   In addition, the treatment of the role played by the Jewish authorities in the reconstructed *Testimonium* does not correspond with
   the Gospels. This passage says the Jewish leaders only "accused"
   Jesus, with Pilate bearing responsibility for having him condemned,
   while the Gospels seem to have the Jewish leaders bear the primary
   responsibility for Jesus's execution.

4. Along these same lines, when stripped of its obvious Christian elements, the *Testimonium* can be read as actually giving a somewhat
   negative assessment of Jesus and the early Christians.[31] For example,
   Josephus seems to be surprised that "the tribe of Christians" had
   not disappeared, despite the shameful end of their leader. As Meier
   notes, there is a distinctly "dismissive if not hostile" tone in this
   line.[32] Not only this, but the word Josephus uses when he notes
   that Jesus "won over" (*epegageto*) Jews and Gentiles can be read
   as having a pejorative connotation. It possibly suggests someone
   duping someone else and thus seems to suggest that this so-called
   Messiah was something of a trickster.[33] These clearly are not things
   a Christian interpolator would have included.

5. This negative tone plausibly explains why early Christian apologists didn't appeal to this passage. Far from supporting the view
   that Jesus was the Messiah, it could be seen as something of an

argument *against* his being the Messiah. This also explains why Origen complains that Josephus does not believe Jesus was the Messiah (*Against Celsus*, 1.45; *Commentary on Matthew*, 10.17). Indeed, as Louis Feldman notes, Origen's complaint actually helps confirm the authenticity of the reconstructed *Testimonium* in that "it makes no sense for Origen to express wonder that Josephus did not admit Jesus to be the Messiah if he did not even mention him."[34]

6. Several other considerations support the authenticity of the reconstructed version of the *Testimonium* as well.[35] For example, shortly after his comments on Jesus, Josephus launches into a much more lengthy discussion of John the Baptist. If the whole of the *Testimonium* was the work of a Christian interpolator, it seems he would have followed the Gospel pattern and placed it *after* the discussion on John the Baptist, whom all Christians regarded as a forerunner of Jesus.[36] It also seems he would have created an account that at least paralleled the discussion of John in terms of length.[37] The fact that the *Testimonium* is short and located before the account of John the Baptist suggests that the Christian interpolator did not take great liberties with Josephus's text but rather simply modified the text slightly in the place he found it.

In light of these considerations, we side with the majority of scholars today who conclude that something like the reconstructed version of the *Testimonium* was penned by Josephus. And this means that this passage confirms a number of central claims of the Gospels. It confirms that Jesus existed, that he was known as a teacher and was generally considered wise, that he was known to have somehow performed surprising feats, that he was crucified under Pilate, and that, surprisingly enough, the movement he began continued on after his death.

Conclusion

We see that, while there is certainly not a wealth of literary evidence corroborating claims found in the Gospels, there is as much, if not more, than we might expect given that the early Jesus movement was a small, obscure sect in the first-century Roman world. The little evidence we do find, however, is significant.

This evidence arguably confirms that Jesus existed (Pliny, Tacitus, Josephus) and had a brother named James, who was killed when Ananus was high priest (Josephus). Jesus was known to be a wonder-worker (Josephus, Celsus), a wise man, and a teacher (Josephus), and he was regarded by his followers as divine (Pliny). He was crucified (Tacitus, Lucian, Josephus) under Pontius Pilate during the reign of Tiberius (Tacitus, Josephus), and his crucifixion seems to have been accompanied by a very long darkness (Thallus). This crucifixion, far from squelching the movement, seems to have been a catalyst for its growth (Tacitus). By AD 49 it was large enough to have incited a riot, resulting in Claudius banishing the Jews from Rome for a while, thus confirming Luke's report in Acts (Suetonius). By the early 60s the movement had become so widespread that Jesus's disciples could be plausibly blamed by Nero for a citywide fire (Tacitus). And by the turn of the century it had spread all the way to Bithynia, where it was large enough to cause problems for the governor (Pliny).

All of this arguably confirms, to some extent at least, the historical veracity of the Gospels. What is perhaps even more interesting, however, is how, even apart from the Gospels, these external sources raise rather forcefully the question we've been asking throughout this work. Namely, how are we to plausibly account for a movement arising in Palestine, within a first-century Jewish context, that was centered on the faith that a recent, wonder-working, wise teacher who had been crucified was actually the saving Messiah and, in fact, the very embodiment of Yahweh himself? Saying that this movement was rooted in a legend simply relabels the problem; it does not solve it.

If we accept the testimony from the early disciples about why they believed what they believed about Jesus, everything is explained. If we don't accept this, however, what plausible explanatory alternative are we left with?

11

Excavating Jesus

The Question of Archaeological Confirmation

The final question customarily asked by historians assessing a document's historical reliability is about the extent to which evidence outside of the document confirms or refutes claims made by the document. More specifically, this last question addresses the relation a document has to other archaeological evidence.[1]

Question 10: Does archaeological evidence corroborate the document?

There has been a significant amount of data arising from archaeological research with respect to ancient Palestine over the last several decades that potentially has implications for our assessment of the historicity of the Gospels. We should point out at the start that, contrary to much popular opinion, archaeology does not usually give us "the hard facts." To the contrary, the meaning and implications of most archaeological artifacts are arguably less self-evident than the meaning and implications of ancient texts. Archaeological artifacts are thus usually (but not always) open to a variety of interpretations and a variety of ways of working out their implications. This intrinsic ambiguity has often been minimized by both Christian apologists and more extreme New Testament critics. Some on both sides have consequently tended to overstate their cases: one side arguing that archaeology "proves" the New Testament to be true, and the other side claiming it "proves" it to be full of historical errors. The reality is that archaeology proves very little—if by *proof* one means something like, "making a case that no reasonable person can deny."

In light of this, we think it best to take an appropriately cautious approach to archaeological findings. In what follows, therefore, we will, with appropriate caution, briefly consider twelve archaeological discoveries, or sets of discoveries, that many scholars argue most strongly confirm aspects of the Gospels or that have implications for our assessment of the historicity of the Gospels.[2]

Evidence of the Nature of First-Century Judaism

In our estimation, one of the most significant lines of archaeological evidence in recent years is that which suggests that first-century Judaism in general, and first-century Palestinian Judaism in particular, remained ardently monotheistic and true to the Torah. As we noted in chapter 2, among the findings that suggest this are the following:

- Coins minted by Herod in first-century Galilee avoid human representations, suggesting that Jews remained sensitive to traditional Jewish interpretations of the second commandment against graven images.
- Material used for ceramic wares in areas heavily populated by Jews consistently conforms to Levitical laws.
- Ritual bathing pools have been discovered throughout the region, suggesting that Jews generally held fast to traditional purity codes.
- A conspicuous absence of pork bones in areas populated by Jews at this time suggests Jews adhered to traditional dietary codes.
- Burial sites in Palestine reflect distinctly Jewish practices.

In our estimation, discoveries such as these provide rather compelling grounds for rejecting the claim of some legendary-Jesus theorists that first-century Palestinian Jews were religiously Hellenized to the point where they naturally would have generated or accepted a legend about a miracle-working God-man.

Bethsaida

Recent excavations of Bethsaida confirm that the Gospel depiction of this city as a fishing village existing on the north shore of the Sea of Galilee is accurate.[3] Also, a jar with a cross was discovered at Bethsaida in 1994 and dates sometime prior to AD 67, lending a confirming note to the witness of Paul and the Gospels, as well as Tacitus and Josephus, that a movement centered on a crucified Messiah existed at this time.[4]

A Galilean Fishing Boat

In 1986 a sunken fishing boat that dates from the first century was found in the Sea of Galilee. Galilean archaeologist Jonathan Reed has noted that this boat, measuring 8.2 by 2.3 meters, "could certainly hold thirteen people," the number of people necessary for Jesus and his twelve disciples to cross the Sea as mentioned a number of times in the Gospels (e.g., Mark 4:36–37).[5] Not only this, but the boat's rather shallow draft (1.2 meters) comports well with Mark's report that, in the midst of a storm, the boat began to founder as it filled with water (Mark 4:37). The boat thus arguably provides confirmation of two aspects of the early Jesus tradition.[6]

The "Pilate Stone"

In 1962 a first-century Latin inscription of the Roman prefect Pontius Pilate dedicating a temple to Tiberius was discovered at Caesarea Maritima, confirming that Pilate reigned in the position ascribed to him by the Gospels.[7] Moreover, by confirming that he was *prefect*, the "Pilate stone," as it has been called, confirms that Pilate would have had the authority to condemn and pardon, as the Gospel accounts report.[8]

A Crucified Man

The entombed remains of a first-century crucified man in Palestine were discovered in 1968. The find confirms aspects of the biblical account of Jesus's crucifixion, including the practice of breaking the legs of crucified criminals (John 19:32–33). It also counts against the argument—yet espoused by Dominic Crossan—that victims of crucifixion wouldn't have been granted a proper burial in a private family tomb, as the Gospel tradition claims for Jesus (Mark 15:42–47).[9]

The Caiaphas Ossuary

In 1990 an ossuary was discovered in a burial cave south of Jerusalem's Old City. The limestone ossuary was uncharacteristically ornate, signaling ownership by a wealthy family. Etched rather crudely into its side in Aramaic was the name "Caiaphas." A number of experts in the field believe that we here have the first archaeological confirmation of an important figure mentioned in the New Testament, namely the high priest who, according to the Gospels, presided over the Jewish trial of Jesus.[10]

The Pool of Siloam

In John's Gospel, Jesus is reported to have healed a blind man by spitting on the ground, mixing up some mud, and rubbing it on his eyes. He then commanded the man to wash his eyes off "in the pool of Siloam" (John 9:1–7). Archaeologists in the early twentieth century had discovered a fifth-century Byzantine church constructed on the site that, at the time, was popularly thought to be the pool of Siloam. In 2004 workers were repairing a broken sewage pipe that carried waste to the Kidron Valley, east of the city of David (southeast of the alternate site). Using heavy equipment to unearth the pipe, they happened to uncover two ancient steps. Fortunately, an archaeologist was working in the area and happened to notice the unearthed steps. He immediately called a halt to the repair work and, with permission from local authorities, had the area turned into an excavation site. What he and others quickly discovered was that these steps led down into a massive pool that they identified as the pool of Siloam. Coins embedded in the plaster of the steps allowed them to date the pool back to the time of Jesus. As James Charlesworth notes, "Scholars have said that there wasn't a Pool of Siloam and that John was using a religious conceit" to illustrate a point. "Now, we have found the Pool of Siloam . . . exactly where John said it was." A Gospel that was thought to be "pure theology is now shown to be grounded in history."[11] With regard to the Gospel of John as a whole, Urban von Wahlde has emphasized this same point recently. Upon investigating twenty different topographical references in John, he concludes that "the intrinsic historicity and accuracy of the references should be beyond doubt."[12]

Peter's House

In Capernaum a simple first-century house was discovered beneath a fourth-century house-church that itself was buried beneath a fifth-century octagonal church structure. Clearly, Christians in the early centuries of church history knew there was something very significant about this first-century house. On the walls of one of the rooms of the first-century structure are inscribed a variety of Christian invocations dating back to the second century. It plausibly suggests this was a residence that was used as a house-church where early Christians gathered. Intriguingly, a number of reputable scholars, ranging across the conservative-liberal spectrum, have concluded that this is likely the house of the apostle Peter, the very building that the Gospels claim Jesus used as a base of operations for his Galilean ministry (Matt. 4:13; 8:14–16; Mark 1:29–35; 2:1).[13]

Jesus's Crucifixion and Burial Sites

Some reputable scholars, including James Charlesworth, argue that we have reasonable grounds for accepting that Jesus was originally buried in a tomb now located beneath the Church of the Holy Sepulchre, very near the place he was crucified.[14] Though the identification of this site as the place where Jesus was crucified and buried goes back to the fourth century, it was routinely dismissed by modern scholars. Among other problems, this site appeared to lie within the city walls, while there is good reason to believe all Jewish crucifixions and burials took place outside the walls (see, e.g., John 19:20; Heb. 13:12). However, more recent archaeological evidence suggests this site would *not* have been within the city walls in the 30s of the first century. Moreover, it appears that several rock-hewn tombs lie at the foundation of the church. For reasons such as this, some scholars suggest it is quite probable that the area upon which the church sits represents the site where Jesus was actually crucified and buried.

Lysanias, Tetrarch of Abilene

Many scholars used to assume that Luke was mistaken when he identified Lysanias as the tetrarch of Abilene around AD 27 (Luke 3:1), for it had earlier been confirmed by archaeology that King Lysanias had been ruler over Chalcis a half century earlier. However, two Greek inscriptions have now revealed the existence of "Lysanias the tetrarch" who reigned in Abilene during the time of Tiberius (AD 14–29), thus confirming the accuracy of Luke's designation.[15] We might add here that in his Gospel and in Acts, Luke mentions a number of titles of officials and local customs that have been confirmed by archaeology. What makes this fact all the more impressive is that these titles frequently changed. Were Luke and his sources not as reliable as they seem to have been, we would have expected him to have gotten these titles wrong a good percentage of the time.

Quirinius, Proconsul of Syria

Related to this, for a long while scholars have questioned the accuracy of Luke's account of the census under the reign of Quirinius (Luke 2:2; cf. Acts 5:37). The reason for this skepticism is that the ancient evidence suggests that Quirinius was not governor of Syria until AD 6. The problem, of course, is that Jesus was born at least ten to twelve years before this time. Hence many scholars have concluded that Luke simply got his facts wrong.

There is a plausible way of resolving this apparent discrepancy even apart from archaeology. Though Luke 2:2 usually is translated something like, "This was the first [prōtos] census that took place while Quirinius was governor," it is possible to translate prōtos not as "first" but as "before." So it is possible Luke is saying that the census that led Joseph and Mary to Bethlehem took place before the census taken under Quirinius in AD 6—the better-known one that caused an uprising.[16] But archaeology offers another way of squaring Luke with the historical evidence. A coin has been discovered that mentions a Quirinius who was proconsul of Syria and Cilicia from 11 BC until after 4 BC, thus reigning at the time of Jesus's birth, as Luke says. It may be, therefore, that the same man ruled twice, or perhaps there were two rulers with this same name.[17]

The James Ossuary

Finally, we should say a brief word about the notorious "James Ossuary." In 2002 an ossuary was discovered with the words, "James, son of Joseph, brother of Jesus," etched on it. Within a short time the ossuary was being countenanced as "the first archaeological link to Jesus and his family."[18] News of this discovery burst onto the scene in November of 2002 with an article by the renowned paleographer Andre Lemaire published in the *Biblical Archaeology Review*. Lemaire concludes his article by arguing that "it seems very probable that this is the ossuary of the James in the New Testament. If so, this would mean that we have here the first epigraphic mention—from about 63 CE—of Jesus of Nazareth."[19] Lemaire's article included a copy of an affirmative assessment of the box completed by the reputable Geological Survey of Israel (Ministry of National Infrastructures).[20] Following this, a team from the Royal Ontario Museum in Toronto examined the ossuary and also determined it to be authentic.

Subsequent inspections have called these original assessments into question, however. The Israel Antiquities Authority (IAA) has argued that, while there is good evidence that the ossuary itself goes back to the first century, part of the inscription is a later forgery.[21] Indeed, they have charged the antiquities collector who brought the box forth with producing the forgery. In a more recent turn of events, Wolfgang Krumbein, of Oldenburg University (Germany), has cast doubts on the findings of the IAA team and has gone as far as to charge them with everything from "errors, biases, mistaken premises, [and] use of inappropriate methodology" to "mistaken geochemistry, defective error control, reliance on unconfirmed data, [and] disregard of information."[22]

Two of the crucial issues dividing experts in the field center on (a) whether the entire inscription reflects an authentic first-century Aramaic script, and (b) whether the patina—the thin covering on the surface of the etching caused by aging—is authentic. The fact that experts in the field have been divided over their assessments of these issues is interesting. It has understandably led some to suspect that factors other than an objective assessment of evidence may be influencing the players in this debate. Obviously, whether the James Ossuary is confirmed to be authentic may have significant religious implications—implications that may be influencing the examiners in one direction or the other.

Moreover, the fact that the James Ossuary emerged, not via careful extraction by an archaeologist from an excavation site, but from the often shady world of the antiquities market, leaves an a priori cloud of suspicion hanging over it in the eyes of many professionals. Thus, on two separate counts—religious and professional—the James Ossuary has found itself caught in the crossfire of turf wars and human emotion. Such a setting is not conducive to a fair and clearheaded assessment of an ancient artifact.[23]

Of course, even if the ossuary's inscription does turn out to be authentic, this doesn't necessarily prove the box held the bones of the brother of Jesus mentioned in the New Testament.[24] On the one hand, it is significant that brothers of the deceased were only mentioned on ossuaries when they were very well-known. One would therefore have to ask oneself how probable it is that there was more than one man *named James* who was the *son of a Joseph* who had a *well-known brother named Jesus* during the rather short interval of time in pre-AD 70 when ossuaries were used in Palestine.

Such considerations lead some scholars, including Lemaire, to conclude that, if the inscription of this ossuary is indeed authentic, it in all probability contained the bones of Jesus's brother.[25] As such, if authentic, the ossuary would confirm that Jesus existed, that he was relatively well-known in the Palestine area in the mid-first century, that his father was known to be Joseph, and that his brother was named James. And these facts would contribute to the difficulty of dismissing the Gospel story of Jesus as substantially legendary. Nonetheless, the issue is at present unsettled, so no firm conclusions can be drawn on this basis.

Conclusion

As we mentioned at the beginning of this chapter, since the meaning of most archaeological artifacts is not self-evident but must be interpreted, archaeology can rarely in and of itself *prove* whether a document is historically reliable. Even the evidence reviewed in this chapter that is generally regarded as offering the most indisputable support for aspects of the Gospels does not *prove* the Gospels are reliable. At the same time, when we consider archaeological evidence alongside all the other reasons we have for concluding that the Gospels are generally reliable, we submit these findings take on a deeper significance. In other words, when seen in light of the other lines of evidence we have considered in this book, the archaeological evidence "goes to pattern," as lawyers sometimes say of courtroom evidence. This evidence gives us yet one more reason to conclude that it is more probable than not that the Gospels are generally reliable and, thus, that their portrait of Jesus is substantially rooted in actual history.

12

Myth Incarnate

The Lord of Legend and Love

Throughout this work we have shown that it is very hard to explain away the Gospels' portrait of Jesus as legendary. First-century Jewish culture was a most unlikely place for a legend about a crucified and resurrected God-man to arise. Evidence from Paul and other sources indicate that this story about Jesus didn't evolve over time, as legends typically do, but rather sprang up virtually overnight. Alleged parallels to the Gospels' Jesus story and the birth of Christianity are, on closer inspection, not impressive. Recent orality studies suggest that oral traditions about Jesus would not have been readily altered with respect to their essential historical integrity. And, on top of all this, the Gospels give us every reason to trust that they are generally reliable when assessed by ordinary historiographical criteria. Thus, as difficult as it may be for some modern people to accept that the Gospels' portrait of Jesus is rooted in history, we submit that it is actually more difficult to accept that it is *not*.

The Reality to Which Myth and Legend Point

We don't want to leave it there, however. Though the Jesus story gives us every reason to believe it is substantially rooted in history, as we've seen, we want to close this work by discussing the curious relationship this historical story has to myth and legend.

The Truth of Mythology

The story of God coming to earth, being born of a virgin, manifesting a heroic, countercultural love toward outcasts, dying for the people who crucified him, and then rising from the dead has a familiar echo to it. If we haven't completely deafened our ears to it, hearing this story has an effect on us that is a bit like recalling a long-forgotten dream. On some level, there's a part of us that seems to intuitively remember something when we come in contact with the loving Savior portrayed in the Gospels. Though it may be suppressed under layers of cynicism and apathy produced by the harshness or sheer monotony of life, and though we may not be able to express it in words, something within us senses that this story puts us in touch with a dream about *the way things are supposed to be*. It reconnects us with something we've lost along the way, something we've perhaps given up on, something we've forgotten.

Throughout history and in every culture, people have, in a wide variety of ways, recalled this dream, even without having had any contact with the Jesus story. They've expressed this dream through myths and legends. We in modern Western culture sometimes respond to unbelievable stories by saying, "Oh, that is *just a myth*." *Myth* and *legend* are for most people equivalent to *untrue*. (Hence the visceral fear some modern Christians have about conceding that anything in the Bible may be myth.) But, as the great mythologist Joseph Campbell has noted, there is a much more profound sense in which myths and legends can be very true. At their best, myths and legends express our innermost sense of reality, our deepest longings, the obstacles we face in pursuing these longings, and our hope that somehow, someday, these longings will be satisfied.[1] In other words, myths and legends express a dream.

We submit that Campbell's observation goes a long way in explaining the curious relationship the Jesus story has with myth and legend. While the Jesus story is, as we have argued, unquestionably grounded in history, this story nevertheless bears a resemblance to certain myths and legends (as was intimated in chapter 4). The resemblance, we submit, is due to the fact that this story *incarnates in actual history* the sense of reality, the longing, the obstacles, and the hopes that many great myths and legends express. In Jesus, God shows his love for the world by becoming a human, serving sinners, dying on a cross, rising from the dead, defeating the devil, rescuing humanity, and giving them eternal life in fellowship with himself. This is the heart of the Jesus story, and it expresses and addresses a dream that is buried in the depths of the human heart.

True Myth Incarnate

While some have tried to use mythic and legendary parallels to argue *against* the historicity of the Jesus story, as we saw in chapter 4, we submit that these vague mythic and legendary parallels are actually what we should *expect* if the Jesus story is indeed *true*—in the fullest sense of the term. After all, one aspect of the Jesus story, extending back into the Old Testament, is the teaching that humans are made in the image of God (Gen. 1:26–28). We're thus "wired" for God, if you will. Not only this, but the New Testament itself declares that Jesus is the "light of all people" (John 1:4, 9) who is always working in the hearts of all people to lead them back to himself (Acts 17:26–28; cf. Rom. 1:19–20).[2] We should thus expect to find echoes of the Jesus story expressed in the myths and legends of various people.

C. S. Lewis expresses this insight when he writes:

Theology, while saying that a special illumination has been vouchsafed to Christians and (earlier) to Jews, also says that there is some divine illumination vouchsafed to all men. . . . We should, therefore, expect to find in the imagination of the great Pagan teachers and myth makers some glimpse of that theme which we believe to be the very plot of the whole cosmic story—the theme of incarnation, death, and rebirth.[3]

The difference between these myths and legends, on the one hand, and the Jesus story, on the other, is not a "difference between falsehood and truth." They are both true but in different senses. As Lewis continues, the difference between them is the difference between a real event on the one hand and dim dreams or premonitions of that same event on the other. It is like watching something come gradually into focus; first it hangs in the clouds of myth and ritual, vast and vague, then it condenses, grows hard and in a sense small, as a historical event in first century Palestine.[4]

This is why Lewis contends that Jesus was "Myth became Fact." In Jesus, "the essential meaning of all things came down from the 'heaven' of myth to the 'earth' of history."[5] The dream expressed in myth and legend, including the premonition of a dying and rising God, is perfectly expressed and becomes historically true in the story of Jesus of Nazareth.

The famous author of the Lord of the Rings trilogy, J. R. R. Tolkien, makes the same point when he says,

> The Gospels contain a fairy-story . . . which embraces all the essence of fairy-stories. They contain many marvels—peculiarly artistic, beautiful, and moving: "mythical" in their perfect, self-contained significance; and among the marvels is the greatest and most complete conceivable eucatastrophe [i.e., a climactic eruption of joy].[6]

Yet the story of Jesus in the New Testament isn't *only* a fairy-story, according to Tolkien, but a fairy-story incarnated in real time and space. In the person of Jesus, an all-embracing fairy-story

> has entered History and the primary world; the desire and aspiration of sub-creation has been raised to the fulfillment of Creation. The Birth of Christ is the eucatastrophe of Man's history. The Resurrection is the eucatastrophe of the story of the Incarnation. The story begins and ends in joy. It has pre-eminently the "inner consistency of reality." There is no tale ever told that men would rather find was true, and none which so many skeptical men have accepted as true on its own merits. . . .
>
> [The Christian] story is supreme; and it is true. Art has been verified. God is the Lord, of angels, and of men—and of elves. Legend and History have met and fused.[7]

What Lewis and Tolkien are saying is that the Jesus story fulfills the intuitions and longings expressed in many myths and legends. The God revealed in the life, death, and resurrection of Jesus Christ is the reality to which certain aspects of various myths and legends point. Jesus is the reality all authors of myths and legends, together with the rest of us, dream of. If we are honest with ourselves, and if we grasp the depth of the good news this story embodies, something quite like the Jesus story is what we hope to be true. Yet, most amazingly, as we've seen throughout this work, this story gives us reason to believe it *is* historically true. We have reason, therefore, to conclude that this story is, at the same time, both *true myth* and *true history*.

The Lord of Legend and Love

We may bring this work to an end by adding one final dimension to our discussion of the innermost dream that Jesus fulfills.

It's All about Love

However secularized people may be, if they have any recollection of the dream that lies buried in their bosom, they sense that somehow the point of everything, if in fact there *is* a point to anything, must have something to do with *love*. Indeed, one could argue that all of our intuitions about morality and the meaning of life are at root an intuition about the supremacy of love. At the core of our being we sense that love is supposed to reign over all. We long for love in all its expressions—intimacy, goodness, and justice—to overcome all its obstacles—isolation, evil, and oppression. This conviction lies behind our ceaseless strivings to make the world a kinder, more just place.

Of course, the worldview people consciously embrace may not be able to make sense of this profound intuition. They may, for example, believe that only physical matter is real and that there is, therefore, no objective reality to moral convictions and no overarching purpose to life. Still, if they are at all emotionally, psychologically, and spiritually healthy, they will *live like* morality *does* objectively exist and as if there *is* a purpose to life, and this purpose has something to do with love. The dream of love reigning supreme is not easily extinguished.

This enduring dream of love has been expressed in myths and legends throughout time. While most love stories are between human lovers (for example, Helen of Troy and Paris, Romeo and Juliet) some are between gods (for example, Ariadne and Dionysus), and some are even between a god and a human (for example, Aphrodite and Adonis). Stories of love between gods have fallen out of favor in recent times in Western secular culture, but extravagant love stories between people obviously abound—James Cameron's 1997 movie, *Titanic*, being one of the more famous examples in recent years. And one still finds an occasional love story of a god (or angel) sacrificing all for the love of a human—Brad Siberling's 1998 movie, *City of Angels*, being one recent instance. Like all legends and myths, these stories express, in a variety of ways, a primordial dream. It is the dream of love that almost unquenchably lies at the heart of every human being.

The Greatest Love Story Ever Told

If the depth of one's love can be measured by the sacrifice one is willing to make for the beloved—and what better indicator of love is there than this?—then the Jesus story must be judged as not only the greatest love story ever told but the greatest love story that *ever could be* told. For this is a story of the all-powerful Creator God making the greatest conceivable sacrifice for a race of people who didn't deserve—or even desire—it. No story could be imagined in which a lover sacrificed more for a beloved who deserved it less. No greater sacrifice, and thus no greater depth of love, could be imagined than this. Indeed, this is a story of *infinite* love, for in this story the lover crosses an infinite distance and pays an infinite price to win a completely undeserving beloved.

In this sense, the Jesus story climaxes and fulfills the dream of all legendary or mythic love stories. To use Tolkien's terminology, this love story embraces the essence of all love stories. It has a "peculiarly artistic, beautiful, and moving" quality to it that is mythical in its perfection. This story thus constitutes "the greatest and most complete conceivable eucatastrophe" found in love stories.[8] All other love stories are approximations of this one.

Yet, as Tolkien and Lewis argued and as we have attempted to demonstrate throughout this book, this love story gives us compelling reasons to conclude that it is not *merely* myth or legend. In the Jesus story we are dealing with real history. We are thus given compelling grounds for concluding that in Jesus, perfect love has "entered History and the primary

Myth Incarnate   153

world." We are given reason to believe that this story is historically true, that our intuitions about love have been verified, and thus that God is more than the "Lord of angels, and of men—and of elves."[9] In the Jesus story we discover that God is also—in fact is first and foremost—the *God of love*.

The Argument from Desire

In fact, the way in which the Jesus story fulfills the mythmaking in-tuitions of the human heart, especially our most fundamental intuition about love, gives us yet one more reason for concluding that this story cannot be merely myth but must rather be rooted in history. For only if this story is historically true can we adequately explain why we long for it—or something like it—to be true. This way of assessing the question does, of course, turn Sigmund Freud's approach to the divine on its head! For here, human longing and desire are read as evidence for a commensurate reality rather than as the creators of merely wish-driven "illusion."[10]

Nature tends not to produce beings who long for things nature itself does not supply. We grow hungry only because there's such a thing as food. We get thirsty only because there's such a thing as water. We have sex drives only because there's such a thing as sex. Human drives and desires seem to point to realities that fulfill them. If we can get philosophi-cal for a moment, we might say that intuitive longings have ontological implications. They tell us something about the real world. In this light we have to ask, What is the reality to which our mythmaking intuitions about and longing for perfect love points? If this is what drives us, what is the reality it is driving us toward?

We submit that in Jesus we find our answer. *If* our Creator is in fact like this—a human being dying a hellish death out of love for those who were killing him—*then* we can begin to understand why we are like we are. Our hope-filled dreams of love get expressed in legend and mythology because they outrun anything we find in the world—and now we can begin to understand why. We dream beyond the world because we are made for someone beyond this world. We are created by God and for God, and as Augustine said, our hearts cannot rest until they rest in God.[11] We are created to love and be loved by a God who is, from eternity to eternity, perfect, unsurpassable, incomprehensible, infinite love.

Paul and the Gospels proclaim that, out of his unfathomable love, the God whom we restlessly long for has come into our world. In Jesus, God entered our domain to fulfill our dreams. He has come to unambiguously reveal *who he is* and *what he is like*. Against everything we've imagined "God" or "the gods" to be, Jesus shows us our Creator is a God who is willing to be crucified to redeem sinners. He has come to reveal to us *who we are*. We are rebels who are nevertheless loved by our Creator with an unconditional love. And he has come to set us free from the power of evil that enslaved us and ultimately to restore the entire creation to what he always wanted it to be. He has come ultimately to extinguish the kingdom of darkness and establish the kingdom of God, in which his perfect love, joy, and peace shall someday reign without opposition.

In our heart of hearts, we want to believe this story is true. And, as we've seen in this book, our minds are now given compelling grounds to accept that this story is, in fact, reflective of actual history. Of course, accepting that this story is rooted in history and placing your trust in Jesus requires faith, for it is impossible to prove *any* historical claim with absolute certainty. However, rejecting the story and basing your life on the assumption that the story is only a myth or a legend also takes faith, for it is equally impossible to prove this claim. What we've attempted to show, however, is that the first act of faith is much more reasonable than the second act of faith.

What will you choose to believe, and how will you choose to live? However you answer this question, you are exercising faith. You are deciding to live your life either on the conviction that the story *is* rooted in history or on the conviction that *it is not*. And while reasons certainly can be given for choosing one option over the other, neither option can be strictly proven (i.e., as one would prove a mathematical equation). However we live, we live by faith. The point of this book has been to persuade readers that choosing to have faith in Jesus, and therefore to live one's life submitted to him as Lord, is the option that is most consistent with the historical evidence and—as we have argued in this chapter—the alternative that makes sense out of, and itself fulfills, the deepest longings of the human heart.

Notes

Introduction

1. C. S. Lewis, *Mere Christianity* (New York: Macmillan, 1943), 56.

2. Throughout this book we will refer to "the portrait" of Jesus found in the New Testament Gospels. In using this term we do not mean to diminish the fact that, along with the many similarities between the Gospels' presentations of Jesus (particularly between the Synoptic Gospels—i.e., Matthew, Mark, and Luke), each of the Gospels offers its own distinctive "portrait" of Jesus. Thus in this last sentence we have referred to the Gospels' "portrait(s)" of Jesus. This nuance should be assumed throughout this work.

3. Generally speaking, we can think of a *legend* as a fictional story that possibly has some rooting in history, while a *myth* is a fictional story that does not. A small minority of scholars hold that the Jesus story is, or at least is more probably, a myth. There is nothing historical about it. Many more, however, hold that while it is at least likely there is a historical core to the Gospels, their portrait of Jesus is shrouded in legend.

4. Along these same lines, we have kept our documentation of secondary sources to a minimum. Those wishing to consult the full range of sources that undergird our conclusions are encouraged to see P. R. Eddy and G. A. Boyd, *The Jesus Legend: A Case for the Historical Reliability of the Synoptic Jesus Tradition* (Grand Rapids: Baker Academic, 2007).

Chapter 1 Miraculous Claims and the Critical Mind

1. For a more comprehensive and in-depth consideration of historiography, the Gospels, and the supernatural, see Eddy and Boyd, *Jesus Legend*, chapter 1.

2. Burton Mack, *A Myth of Innocence: Mark and Christian Origins* (Philadelphia: Fortress, 1988), 23. For a critique of Mack's naturalistic explanation of early Christianity, see G. A. Boyd, *Cynic Sage or Son of God?* (Wheaton: Victor/BridgePoint, 1995).

3. Robert Funk, "Twenty-one Theses," *The Fourth R* (July–August 1998): 8. For a response to the charge that miracles are an affront to the justice and integrity of God, see G. A. Boyd, *Is God to Blame? Moving Beyond Pat Answers to the Problem of Evil* (Downers Grove, IL: InterVarsity, 2003).

4. John Dominic Crossan, *Jesus: A Revolutionary Biography* (San Francisco: HarperSanFrancisco, 1994), 94–95.

5. See, for example, R. G. Collingwood, *The Idea of History* (Oxford: Clarendon, 1946), 139.

6. For an introductory-level discussion of the way in which quantum physics and other areas of contemporary science disclose a probalistic, "open-ended" dimension to reality, see G. Boyd, *The Cosmic Dance: What the New Scientific Revelation Can Teach Us about Life, Freedom and the Nature of Time* (forthcoming).

7. On the principle of analogy, see Wolfhart Pannenberg, "Redemptive Event and History," in *Basic Questions in Theology: Collected Essays*, vol. 1, trans. George H. Kehm (Philadelphia: Fortress, 1970), 39–53; T. Peters, "The Use of Analogy in Historical Method," *Catholic Biblical Quarterly* 35 (1973): 475–82.

8. On how widespread the belief and experience of "spirit possession" is within primordial cultures, see E. Bourguignon, "Spirit Possession Belief and Social Structure," in *The Realm of the Extra-Human: Ideas and Actions*, ed. A. Bharatic (Paris: Mouton, 1976), 19.

9. A 1995 *Time* magazine poll found that 69 percent of Americans believe in miracles; see J. Bonfante et al., "The Message of Miracles," *Time* (April 10, 1995), 65. In a startling poll, it was found that when it comes to belief in "paranormal phenomena . . . better-educated people are actually more likely to believe"; T. W. Rice, "Believe It or Not: Religious and Other Paranormal Beliefs in the United States," *Journal for the Scientific Study of Religion* 42 (2003): 95–106 (quotes from pp. 98, 101). See also N. Gibbs, "Angels among Us," *Time* (December 27, 1993), 56–65; G. Gallup Jr., and J. Castelli, *The People's Religion: American Faith in the 90s* (New York: Macmillan, 1989).

10. See, for example, G. E. Marcus and D. Cushman, "Ethnographies as Texts," *Annual Review of Anthropology* 11 (1982):

25–69; J. R. Bowlin and P. G. Stromberg, "Representation and Reality in the Study of Culture," *American Anthropologist* 99 (1997): 123–34; R. Feleppa, "Emics, Etics, and Social Objectivity," *Current Anthropology* 27 (1986): 243–55.

11. Bowlin and Stromberg put the matter starkly: "It should regularly occur that good ethnography encourages us to conclude that beliefs and warrants held by members of another society track the truth better than our own. An ethnography sufficiently humble about matters of belief must concede this possibility and should regard this kind of critical revision of our own beliefs as a welcome consequence of careful inquiry." Bowlin and Stromberg, "Representation and Reality," 130.

12. For example, Jamie Bulatao claims that, while he believes most cases of purported demonic possession can be explained in naturalistic/psychological terms, he has personally encountered four cases in which the demonic phenomena "was not only occurring inside the person but actually manifested itself by external events" that seemed inexplicable in natural terms—including the hurling of stones by an apparently unseen force. He justifiably concludes that "these phenomena present a challenge to human understanding." Jamie Bulatao, "Local Cases of Possession and Their Cure," *Philippine Studies* 30 (1982): 424–25. See also M. Scott Peck's recent book, *Glimpses of the Devil: A Psychiatrist's Personal Accounts of Possession, Exorcism and Redemption* (New York: Free Press, 2005), which includes descriptions of two exorcisms in which he was personally involved. For Edith Turner's (wife and colleague of the famed anthropologist Vic Turner) experience in Africa of an exorcism involving seemingly impossible phenomena (by Western scientific standards), see Edith Turner, *Experiencing Ritual: A New Interpretation of African Healing* (Philadelphia: University of Pennsylvania Press, 1992), 149–50; and especially, Edith Turner, "The Reality of Spirits," *ReVision* 15, no. 1 (1992):

28. See also L. Peters, *Ecstasy and Healing in Nepal* (Malibu, CA: Undena, 1981); J. T. Houk, *Spirit, Drums and Blood: The Orishi Religion in Trinidad* (Philadelphia: Temple University Press, 1995), 4; J. Favret-Saada, *Deadly Words: Witchcraft in the Bocage*, trans. C. Cullen (Cambridge: Cambridge University Press, 1980), 22.

Such phenomena are witnessed by Western academics more frequently than one would infer from the academic literature. As some of them have noted, fear of being ostracized by the academic community makes many hesitant to report their experiences. See P. Stoller, "Eye, Mind, and Word in Anthropology," *L'Homme* 24 (1984): 93; P. Stoller, "Beatitudes, Beasts, and Anthropological Burdens," *Medical Anthropology Newsletter* 13 (August 1982): 2; L. Ramanucci-Ross, "On Analyses of Event Structures as Philosophical Derivations of the Investigating Cultures," in *Essays in Humanistic Anthropology*, ed. B. Grindal and D. Warren (Washington, DC: University Press of America, 1979), 57–58, 60.

Chapter 2 A Most Unexpected Legend

1. For a more comprehensive and in-depth consideration of these matters, see Eddy and Boyd, *Jesus Legend*, chapter 2.

2. L. Hurtado, *How on Earth Did Jesus Become a God? Historical Questions about Earliest Devotion to Jesus* (Grand Rapids: Eerdmans, 2005), 42.

3. See H. Shanks, "Synagogue Excavation Reveals Stunning Mosaic of Zodiac and Torah Ark," *Biblical Archaeological Review* 10, no. 3 (1984): 32–44; J. H. Charlesworth, "Jewish Astrology in the Talmud, Pseudepigrapha, the Dead Sea Scrolls, and Early Palestinian Synagogues," *Harvard Theological Review* 70 (1977): 193–98.

4. See G. Paterson Corrington, *The Divine Man: His Origin and Function in Hellenistic Popular Religion* (New York: Lang, 1986), 181–93.

5. See Charlesworth, "Jewish Astrology," 195, 198; Shanks, "Synagogue Excavation," 39. The definitive study on the Tiberias synagogue is M. Dothan, *Hammath Tiberias—Early Synagogues and the Hellenistic and Roman Remains* (Jerusalem: Israel Exploration Society, University of Haifa, 1983).

6. See E. E. Urbach, "The Rabbinical Laws of Idolatry in the Second and Third Centuries in the Light of Archaeological and Historical Facts," *Israel Exploration Journal* 9 (1959): 237; Dothan, *Hammath Tiberias*, 48–50; M. Avi Yonah, "The Caesarea Inscription of the Twenty-Four Priestly Courses," in *The Teachers Yoke: Studies in Memory of Henry Trantham* (Dallas: Baylor University Press, 1968), 46–57; R. Hachlili, "The Zodiac in Ancient Jewish Art: Representation and Significance," *Bulletin of American Schools of Oriental Research* 228 (1977): 61–77.

7. See L. W. Hurtado, "First-Century Jewish Monotheism," *Journal for the Study of the New Testament* 71 (1998): 3–26, especially 5–8; R. Bauckham, *God Crucified: Monotheism and Christology in the New Testament* (Grand Rapids: Eerdmans, 1999), 11.

8. See C. Holladay, *Theios Aner in Hellenistic Judaism: A Critique of the Use of This Category in New Testament Christology* (Missoula, MT: Scholars Press, 1977), 195; D. L. Tiede, *The Charismatic Figure as Miracle Worker* (Missoula, MT: Scholars Press, 1972), 134, 245–46; B. Blackburn, *Theios Aner and the Markan Miracle Traditions* (Tübingen, Germany: Mohr-Siebeck, 1991), 229–32.

9. Holladay, *Theios aner*, 238. See also Bauckham, *God Crucified*, 17; and L. W. Hurtado, *One God, One Lord: Early Christian Devotion and Ancient Jewish Monotheism* (Philadelphia: Fortress, 1988), 51–69.

10. See T. Rajak, "The Hasmoneans and the Uses of Hellenism," in *A Tribute to Geza Vermes: Essays on Jewish and Christian Literature and History*, ed. P. R. Davies and R. T. White (Sheffield, UK: Sheffield Academic Press, 1990), 265; F. Millar,

"Empire, Community and Culture in the Roman Near East: Greeks, Syrians, Jews and Arabs," *Journal of Jewish Studies* 38 (1987): 143–64; F. Millar, "The Problem of Hellenistic Syria," in *Hellenism in the East*, ed. A. Kuhrt and S. Sherwin-White (London: Routledge, 1987), 110–33; P. Green, *Alexander to Actium: The Historical Evolution of the Hellenistic Age* (Berkeley: University of California Press, 1990), 312–35.

11. See G. W. Bowersock, "Paganism and Greek Culture," in *Hellenism in Late Antiquity* (Ann Arbor: University of Michigan Press, 1990), 7.

12. A. T. Kraabel, "Paganism and Judaism: The Sardis Evidence," in *Melanges offerts a Marcel Simon: Paganisme, Judaisme, Christianisme, influences et affrontements dans le monde antique* (Paris: de Boccard, 1978), 13–33.

13. L. L. Grabbe, *Judaism from Cyrus to Hadrian*, vol. 1, *The Persian and Greek Periods* (Minneapolis: Fortress, 1992), 170.

14. As Hengel notes, evidence suggests Jews generally were more inclined toward absorbing elements of Greek religion and culture prior to the Maccabean revolt in 168 BC than they were after this revolt; M. Hengel, "Judaism and Hellenism Revisited," in *Hellenism in the Land of Israel*, ed. J. J. Collins and G. E. Sterling (Notre Dame: University of Notre Dame Press, 2001), 29.

15. For discussion, see M. Hengel, "Judaism and Hellenism Revisted," with C. Marckschies, *The "Hellenization" of Judea in the First Century after Christ* (Philadelphia: Trinity, 1989), 54.

16. S. Freyne, "Galilee-Jerusalem Relations According to Josephus' *Life*," *New Testament Studies* 33 (1987): 607.

17. J. L. Reed, "Galilean Archaeology and the Historical Jesus," in *Jesus Now and Then: Images of Jesus in History and Christology*, ed. M. Meyer and C. Hughes (Harrisburg, PA: Trinity, 2001), 118–19.

18. Ibid., 117.

19. See ibid., 117; M. Chancey and E. M. Meyer, "How Jewish Was Sepphoris in Jesus' Time?" *Biblical Archaeology Review* 26 (2000): 25–27.

20. J. L. Reed, "The Identity of the Galileans," in *Archaeology and the Galilean Jesus: A Re-examination of the Evidence* (Harrisburg, PA: Trinity, 2000), 44, 47, 49; B. Hesse and P. Wapnish, "Can Pig Remains Be Used for Ethnic Diagnosis in the Ancient Near East?" in *The Archaeology of Israel: Constructing the Past, Interpreting the Present*, ed. N. Silberman and D. Small (Sheffield, UK: Sheffield Academic Press, 1997), 238–70.

21. E. M. Meyer, "The Challenge of Hellenism for Early Judaism and Christianity," *Biblical Archaeologist* 55 (June 1992): 88.

22. S. Freyne, *Galilee: From Alexander the Great to Hadrian, 323 B.C.E. to 135 C.E.: A Study of Second Temple Judaism* (Wilmington, DE: Glazier, 1980), 143–44.

23. Meyer, "Challenge of Hellenism," 88.

24. For his discussion of Second Temple Jewish beliefs on resurrection, see N. T. Wright, *The Resurrection of the Son of God* (Minneapolis: Fortress, 2003), 129–206.

Chapter 3 "Long, Long Ago and Far, Far Away?"

1. For a more comprehensive consideration of the matters discussed in this chapter, see Eddy and Boyd, *Jesus Legend*, chapter 5.

2. Many scholars doubt that Paul wrote all the letters attributed to him in the New Testament. For our purposes, however, nothing of any consequence hangs on this debate. On the authorship of the disputed epistles, see I. H. Marshall, "Recent Study of the Pastoral Epistles," *Themelios* 23 (1997): 3–29.

3. On the deity of Christ in Paul's theology, see the relevant sections in M. J. Harris, *Jesus as God: The New Testament Use of Theos in Reference to Jesus* (Grand Rapids: Baker, 1992); D. P. Capes, *Old Testament Yahweh Texts in Paul's Christology* (Tübingen: Mohr Siebeck, 1992); L. W. Hurtado, *Lord Jesus Christ: Devotion to Jesus in Earli-*

est Christianity (Grand Rapids: Eerdmans, 2003), 98–153.

4. R. Bauckham, *God Crucified: Monotheism and Christology in the New Testament* (Grand Rapids: Eerdmans, 1999), viii.

5. G. A. Wells, *The Historical Evidence of Jesus* (Buffalo, NY: Prometheus Books, 1982), 22.

6. E. Doherty, *The Jesus Puzzle: Did Christianity Begin with a Mythical Christ?* (Ottawa: Canadian Humanist, 1999), 30.

7. On the reliability of Acts, see especially C. J. Hemer, *The Book of Acts in the Setting of Hellenistic History*, ed. C. H. Gempf (Winona Lake, IN: Eisenbauns, 1990); and C. Keener's forthcoming two-volume commentary on Acts to be published by Eerdmans.

8. See E. Bakker, "Activation and Preservation: The Interdependence of Text and Performance in an Oral Tradition," *Oral Tradition* 8 (1993): 5–20; J. M. Foley, *Immanent Art: From Structure to Meaning in Traditional Oral Epic* (Bloomington: Indiana University Press, 1991), especially 5–13; J. M. Foley, "Selection as *pars pro toto*: The Role of Metonymy in Epic Performance and Tradition," in *The Kalevala and the World's Traditional Epics*, ed. L. Honko (Helsinki: Finnish Literature Society, 2002), 106–27. We will discuss this topic further in chapter 9.

9. This phenomenon is well documented in a wide variety of settings; see, e.g., H. J. Becken, "The Use of Oral Tradition in Historiography: Some Pitfalls and Challenges," *Studia historiae eclesiasticae* 19 (1993): 87; I. Okpewho, *African Oral Literature: Backgrounds, Character, and Continuity* (Bloomington: Indiana University Press, 1992), 183, 192; J. A. Robinson, "Personal Narratives Reconsidered," *Journal of American Folklore* 94 (1981): 72; E. Tonkin, "The Boundaries of History in Oral Performance," *History in Africa* 9 (1982): 278.

10. Wells, *Historical Evidence*, 168.

11. See Eddy and Boyd, *Jesus Legend*, 212–14.

12. Ibid., 215–16.

Chapter 4 Rising Gods, Legendary Heroes, and Divinized Teachers

1. For a more comprehensive consideration of the matters discussed in this chapter, see Eddy and Boyd, *Jesus Legend*, chapter 3.

2. For a discussion of the various Greco-Roman gods who can be used to explain the rise of the Christ cult, see R. M. Price, *Deconstructing Jesus* (Amherst, NY: Prometheus, 2000), 86–92.

3. For a brief history of the hero myth theory, see Robert A. Segal, "Introduction: In Quest of the Hero," in Otto Rank, Lord Raglan, and Alan Dundes, *In Quest of the Hero* (Princeton: Princeton University Press, 1990), vii–xli. Legendary-Jesus theorist Robert Price goes so far as to argue that "every detail of the [Christ] story fits the mythic hero archetype, with nothing left over." From this Price surmises that it is "arbitrary to assert that there must have been a historical figure lying in back of the myth." Robert Price, "Christ a Fiction" (1997) available online at http://www.infidels.org/library/modern/robert_price/fiction.html (accessed December 15, 2005).

4. J. Z. Smith, "Dying and Rising Gods," in *Encyclopedia of Religion*, ed. M. Eliade, vol. 4, (New York: Macmillan, 1987), 521. For a detailed critique of the "dying and rising gods" thesis, see Eddy and Boyd, *Jesus Legend*, 142–46.

5. Charles E. Murgia, "Response [to Dundes]," in *Protocol of the Twenty-fifth Colloquy, Center for Hermeneutical Studies in Hellenistic and Modern Culture, 12 December 1976* (Berkeley, CA: Center for Hermeneutical Studies in Hellenistic and Modern Culture, 1977), 52. On Lincoln, see Francis Lee Utley, "Lincoln Wasn't There, or Lord Raglan's Hero," *CEA Chap Book* (Washington, DC: College English Association, 1965; supplement to *The CEA Critic* 22, June 1965).

6. On Apollonius, see F. C. Conybeare, ed., *Philostratus: The Life of Apollonius of Tyana*, 2 vols. (Cambridge: Harvard University Press, 1912); M. Dzielska, *Apollonius of Tyana in Legend and History* (Rome: L'erma, 1986).

7. See R. Bauckham, "The Eyewitnesses and the Gospel Tradition," *Journal for the Study of the Historical Jesus* 1 (2003): 28–60; and especially R. Bauckham, *Jesus and the Eyewitnesses: The Gospels as Eyewitness Testimony* (Grand Rapids: Eerdmans, 2006).

8. On Sabbatai Sevi, see W. D. Davies, "From Schweitzer to Scholem: Reflections on Sabbatai Svi," *Journal of Biblical Literature* 95 (1976): 529–58; and especially G. G. Scholem, *Sabbatai Sevi: The Mystic Messiah, 1626–1676*, trans. R. J. Zwi Werblowsky (1957; repr., Princeton: Princeton University Press, 1973).

9. Scholem, *Sabbatai Sevi*, 238.

10. On Simon Kimbangu, see M. L. Martin, *Kimbangu: An African Prophet and His Church*, trans. D. M. Moore (Grand Rapids: Eerdmans, 1975); S. Rabey, "The People's Prophet," *Christian History* 32, no. 3 (2003): 32–34.

11. On Jesus's sense of self-identity, see B. Witherington, *The Christology of Jesus* (Minneapolis: Fortress, 1990); N. T. Wright, *Jesus and the Victory of God* (Minneapolis: Fortress, 1996), especially chapter 13.

Chapter 5 Oral Traditions and Legend-Making

1. For a more comprehensive consideration of the matters discussed in this chapter, see Eddy and Boyd, *Jesus Legend*, chapters 6–7.

2. Skepticism about Greco-Roman literacy rates has been intensified in recent years by the work of W. V. Harris, *Ancient Literacy* (Cambridge: Harvard University Press, 1989). See also M. Bar-Ilan, "Illiteracy in the Land of Israel in the First Centuries C.E.," in *Essays in the Social Scientific Study of Judaism and Jewish Society*, vol. 2, ed. S. Fishbane and S. Schoenfeld (Hoboken, NJ: KTAV, 1992), 55. This skeptical approach has been applied to Roman Palestine by C. Hezser, *Jewish Literacy in Roman Palestine* (Tübingen, Germany: Mohr-Siebeck, 2001). For a much more optimistic assessment of Palestinian literacy rates in the day of Jesus, see A. Millard, *Reading and Writing in the Time of Jesus* (Sheffield, UK: Sheffield Academic Press, 2000).

3. A. K. Bowman, "Literacy in the Roman Empire: Mass and Mode," in *Literacy in the Roman World*, ed. M. Beard (Ann Arbor: University of Michigan Press, 1991), 123–27; N. Horsfall, "Statistics or States of Mind?" in Beard, ed., *Literacy in the Roman World*, 59.

4. See, for example, the discovery of inexpensive, perhaps even free, writing materials used by soldiers at Vindolanda. A. K. Bowman and J. D. Thomas, "Vindolanda 1985: The New Writing-Tablets," *Journal of Roman Studies* 76 (1986): 120–23; A. K. Bowman and J. D. Thomas, "New Texts from Vindolanda," *Britannia* 18 (1987): 125–42; and especially A. K. Bowman, *Life and Letters on the Roman Frontier: Vindolanda and Its People* (London: British Museum Press, 1994). See also Bowman, "Literacy in the Roman Empire," 128.

5. See, for example, Bowman, "Literacy in the Roman Empire," 121–22; A. E. Hanson, "Ancient Illiteracy," in Beard, ed., *Literacy in the Roman World*, 164; Alan Millard, "The Practice of Writing in Ancient Israel," *Biblical Archaeologist* 35 (1972): 98–111; Alan Millard, "An Assessment of the Evidence for Writing in Ancient Israel," in *Biblical Archaeology Today: Proceedings of the International Congress on Biblical Archaeology, Jerusalem, April 1984*, ed. Janet Amitai (Jerusalem: Israel Exploration Society, 1985), 301–12.

6. J. P. Meier, *A Marginal Jew: Rethinking the Historical Jesus*, vol. 1, *The Roots of the Problem and the Person* (New York: Doubleday, 1991), 275.

7. Birger Gerhardsson, "The Gospel Tradition," in *The Interrelations of the Gospels*, ed. David L. Dungan (Leuven, Belgium: Peeters, 1990), 538.

8. Papias's report is recorded by Eusebius in his *Church History*, 3.39.16. For a forceful defense of Papias's testimony as deriving from the apostle John, see R. H. Gundry, *Mark: A Commentary on His Apology for the Cross* (Grand Rapids: Eerdmans, 1993), 1026–45.

9. Lauri Honko, "Introduction: Oral and Semiliterary Epics," in *The Epic: Oral and Written*, ed. L. Honko, J. Handoo, and J. M. Foley (Mysore, India: Central Institute of Indian Languages, 1998), 9.

10. Honko himself has witnessed one oral narrative that took seven days to complete. See Lauri Honko, *Textualizing the Siri Epic* (Helsinki, Finland: Academia Scientiarum Fennica, 1998), 15.

11. See ibid., 193–94. Honko refers to the broader narrative as "the mental text." Each particular oral performance, whether written out (as with the Gospels) or not, presupposes the whole narrative and expresses a part of this broader narrative. In chapter 9 we will see how understanding this dimension of orally dominant cultures affects our estimation of the differences between the Gospels.

12. Richard Dorson, "Introduction: Folklore and Traditional History," in *Folklore and Traditional History*, ed. R. Dorson (The Hague and Paris: Mouton, 1973), 9.

13. Patrick Pender-Cudlip, "Oral Traditions and Anthropological Analysis: Some Contemporary Myths," *Azania* 7 (1972): 12; see also J. C. Miller, "Introduction: Listening for the African Past," in *The African Past Speaks: Essays on Oral Tradition and History*, ed. J. C. Miller (Hamden, CT: Archon, 1980), 51.

14. Miller, "Listening for the African Past," 51–52.

15. See, for example, Annikki Kaivola-Bregenhoj, "Varying Folklore," in *Thick Corpus, Organic Variation and Textuality in Oral Tradition*, ed. Lauri Honko (Helsinki, Finland: Finnish Literature Society, 2000), 101; Ruth Finnegan, *Oral Literature in Africa* (1970; repr., Nairobi: Oxford University Press, 1979), 370.

16. See, for example, J. Handoo, "People Are Still Hungry for Kings: Folklore and Oral History," in *Dynamics of Tradition: Perspectives on Oral Poetry and Folk Belief*, ed. L. Tarkka (Helsinki, Finland: Finnish Literature Society, 2003), 70.

17. R. H. Stein, *The Synoptic Problem: An Introduction* (Grand Rapids: Baker, 1987), 191.

18. James D. J. Dunn, *Christianity in the Making*, vol. 1, *Jesus Remembered* (Grand Rapids: Eerdmans, 2003), 176.

19. Ibid., 177–80.

20. On the importance of individual "strong tradition bearers" in orally dominant communities, see J. D. Niles, *Homo Narrans: The Poetics and Anthropology of Oral Literature* (Philadelphia: University of Pennsylvania Press, 1999), 173–93.

21. See Bauckham, "Eyewitnesses and the Gospel Tradition," 28–60. Although it is not available at the time of this writing, Bauckham's book-length treatment of the topic of eyewitness tradition in the Gospels should be a groundbreaking work that will serve to open up lines of fresh inquiry on this matter. See Bauckham, *Jesus and the Eyewitnesses*.

22. Cf. also John 3:26, 28; 5:32; Acts 1:8, 22; 2:32; 3:15; 5:32; 10:37–41; 13:31; 22:15, 18; 23:11; 26:16; Rom. 1:9; 1 Cor. 1:6; 15:6; 2 Cor. 1:23; Phil. 1:8; 1 Thess. 2:5, 10; 1 Tim. 6:12–13; 2 Tim. 2:2; 1 Peter 5:1; 2 Peter 1:16; 1 John 5:6–11; Rev. 1:5; 2:13; 3:14; 6:9; 11:3; 17:6.

23. Stein, *Synoptic Problem*, 193.

Part 2 The Gospels and Ten Tests of Historical Reliability

1. These questions and concerns are methodological commonplaces within the field of historiography. See, e.g., R. J. Shafer,

ed., *A Guide to Historical Method* (1969; rev. ed., Homewood, IL: Dorsey, 1974), 157–58; L. Gottschalk, *Understanding History: A Primer on Historical Method* (New York: Knopf, 1963), 150; G. J. Renier, *History: Its Purpose and Method* (New York: Harper & Row, 1950), 108–10, 162–65.

Chapter 6 Following the Paper Trail

1. For more thorough considerations of these two questions, see Eddy and Boyd, *Jesus Legend*, chapter 8 ("The Genre and Nature of the Canonical Gospels") and the "Textual Criticism" section in chapter 9.

2. These include papyri, uncials, minuscules, and lectionaries. On the extant Greek manuscripts, see M. W. Holmes, "Textual Criticism," in *Interpreting the New Testament: Essays on Methods and Issues*, ed. D. A. Black and D. S. Dockery (Nashville: Broadman & Holman, 2001), 48–49; B. M. Metzger, *The Text of the New Testament: Its Transmission, Corruption and Restoration*, 2nd ed. (1964; repr., New York: Oxford University Press, 1968), 36–67; K. Aland and B. Aland, *The Text of the New Testament*, 2nd ed., trans. E. F. Rhodes (1987; repr., Grand Rapids: Eerdmans, 1989), 72–184; and J. K. Elliott, *A Bibliography of Greek New Testament Manuscripts*, 2nd ed. (1989; repr., New York: Cambridge University Press, 2000).

3. For a summary of extant early translations and patristic citations, see Holmes, "Textual Criticism," 49–50; Metzger, *Text of the New Testament*, 67–92; Aland and Aland, *Text of the New Testament*, 171–221.

4. On these comparisons with other ancient texts, see Metzger, *Text of the New Testament*, 34; E. J. Epp, "Textual Criticism," in *The New Testament and Its Modern Interpreters*, ed. E. J. Epp and G. W. MacRae (Philadelphia: Fortress, 1989), 91; F. F. Bruce, *The New Testament Documents: Are They Reliable?* (Downers Grove, IL: InterVarsity, 1960), 16. Metzger offers some relevant thoughts in an interview; see L. Strobel, *The*

Case for Christ: A Journalist's Personal Investigation of the Evidence for Jesus (Grand Rapids: Zondervan, 1998), 57–66.

5. This is the famous John Rylands' papyrus fragment ($\mathfrak{P}^{52}$).

6. Metzger, *Text of the New Testament*, 34; Epp, "Textual Criticism," 91.

7. See especially D. R. MacDonald, *The Homeric Epics and the Gospel of Mark* (New Haven: Yale University Press, 2000); also D. R. MacDonald, "Secrecy and Recognition in the *Odyssey* and Mark: Where Wrede Went Wrong," in *Ancient Fiction and Early Christian Narrative*, ed. R. F. Hock, J. B. Chance, and J. Perkins (Atlanta: Scholars Press, 1998), 139–53; D. R. MacDonald, *Does the New Testament Imitate Homer? Four Case Studies from the Acts of the Apostles* (New Haven: Yale University Press, 2003).

8. M. M. Mitchell, "Homer in the New Testament," *Journal of Religion* 83 (2003): 253. MacDonald alludes to the possible parallels with the Jonah story in a footnote but unfortunately focuses all his attention on Homer.

9. S. Sandmel, "Parallelomania," *Journal of Biblical Literature* 81 (1962): 1–13. See also M. Hooker's review of MacDonald's book in *Journal of Theological Studies* 53 (2002): 198.

10. MacDonald, *Homeric Epics*, 7.

11. E.g., ibid., 171.

12. For helpful discussions of oral versus written "registers" or "conceptions," see E. J. Bakker, "How Oral Is Oral Composition?" in *Signs of Orality: The Oral Tradition and Its Influence in the Greek and Roman World*, ed. E. A. MacKay (Boston: Brill, 1999), 29–37; J. M. Foley, "Oral Tradition into Textuality," in *Texts and Textuality: Textual Instability, Theory and Interpretation*, ed. P. Cohen (New York: Garland, 1997), 1–24; J. M. Foley, "What's in a Sign?" in *Signs of Orality*, ed. MacKay, 1–27.

13. C. A. Evans, "Midrash," in *Dictionary of Jesus and the Gospels*, ed. J. B. Green, S. McKnight, and I. H. Marshall (Downers Grove, IL: InterVarsity, 1992), 546.

14. See, for example, E. Doherty, "The Gospels as Midrash and Symbolism," in Doherty, *Jesus Puzzle*, especially 225–39.

15. D. I. Brewer, *Techniques and Assumptions in Jewish Exegesis before 70 CE* (Tübingen, Germany: Mohr-Siebeck, 1992).

16. G. W. Dawes, "Why Historicity Still Matters: Raymond Brown and the Infancy Narratives," *Pacifica* 19 (2006): 174. While Dawes is referring here specifically to the infancy narratives, one can legitimately apply his insight to the range of historically oriented narratives found in the Gospels.

Chapter 7 Who, When, and Why?

1. For a more comprehensive look at these two questions, see the relevant sections in chapter 9 of Eddy and Boyd, *Jesus Legend*.

2. As noted by N. T. Wright, *The New Testament and the People of God* (Minneapolis: Fortress, 1992), 423.

3. The excerpt is found in Eusebius's *Ecclesiastical History*, 3.39.15. We have used the translation found in Joel Marcus, *Mark 1–8* (New York: Doubleday, 2000), 21–22. Many have argued that the "John" whom Papias was in touch with was not the apostle John, but we find the evidence for the apostle John to be compelling. See C. S. Keener, *The Gospel of John: A Commentary*, vol. 1 (Peabody, MA: Hendrikson, 2003), 95–98; and especially Gundry, *Mark*, 1026–45.

4. Irenaeus, *Against Heresies*, 3.1.2 (ca. 180); Tertullian, *Against Marcion*, 4.5 (ca. 200); Clement of Alexandria, *Hypotyposes* (ca. 200) (according to Eusebius, *Ecclesiastical History*, 6.14.5–7).

5. Excerpt from *Ecclesiastical History*, 3.39.16. The passage is notoriously difficult to translate. See the discussion in H. Koester, *Ancient Christian Gospels: Their History and Development* (Philadelphia: Trinity, 1990), 316; and D. A. Carson, D. Moo, and L. Morris, *An Introduction to the New Testament* (Grand Rapids: Zondervan, 1992), 68.

6. Irenaeus, quoted in Eusebius, *Ecclesiastical History*, 5.8.2; translation taken from Koester, *Ancient Christian Gospels*, 317.

7. Eusebius, *Ecclesiastical History*, 6.25.4.

8. Irenaeus, *Against Heresies*, 1.25.1; translation taken from Koester, *Ancient Christian Gospels*, 334.

9. Eusebius, *Ecclesiastical History*, 5.8.3; translation taken from Koester, *Ancient Christian Gospels*, 335.

10. For the Greek text and an English translation, see R. G. Heard, "The Old Gospel Prologues," *Journal of Theological Studies* 6 (1955): 7.

11. Irenaeus, *Against Heresies*, 2.1.2.

12. Eusebius, *The History of the Church*, trans. G. A. Williamson (New York: Penguin, 1965), 254–55.

13. So argues Martin Hengel, "The Titles of the Gospels and the Gospel of Mark," in *Studies in the Gospel of Mark*, trans. John Bowden (Philadelphia: Fortress, 1985), 67–72.

14. Ibid., 74–81.

15. For the case for dating the Gospels and the New Testament as a whole before AD 70, see J. A. T. Robinson, *Redating the New Testament* (Philadelphia: Westminster, 1976). Marice Casey has argued for a dating for Mark in the mid-30s; see Marice Casey, *Aramaic Sources of Mark's Gospel* (New York: Cambridge University Press, 1998), 259–60. A similar argument is made by James G. Crossley, *The Date of Mark's Gospel: Insight from the Law in Earliest Christianity* (New York: Clark, 2004), 206–9. E. E. Ellis has argued for a mid-50s date; see E. E. Ellis, "The Date and Provenance of Mark's Gospel," in *The Four Gospels 1992: Festschrift Frans Neirynck*, vol. 2, ed. F. Van Segbroeck et al. (Leuven, Belgium: Leuven University Press, 1992), 814.

16. Robert Funk, "On Distinguishing Historical from Fictive Narrative," *Forum* 9 (1993): 191.

17. For example, the scholars who participated in the Acts Seminar concluded

that, "In the Gospel of Luke, the author's use of Mark often involved creating new stories to fit his theological program"; "The Acts Seminar: Voting Records, Fall 2002," *Forum* (n.s.) 5 (2002): 118.

18. This illustration is all the more surprising since Kelber is among those relatively few New Testament scholars who consistently *appreciate* the significance of orality studies for understanding the Gospels.

19. See W. Kelber, *The Kingdom in Mark: A New Place and a New Time* (Philadelphia: Fortress, 1974); and especially W. Kelber, *The Oral and the Written Gospel: The Hermeneutics of Speaking and Writing in the Synoptic Tradition, Mark, Paul, and Q* (Philadelphia: Fortress, 1983), 97, 130.

20. See the argument in T. E. Boomershine, "Peter's Denial as Polemic or Confession: The Implications of Media Criticism for Biblical Hermeneutics," *Semeia* 39 (1987): 59.

21. See R. Thomas, *Oral Tradition and Written Record in Classical Athens* (New York: Cambridge University Press, 1989), 93–94.

22. On the anachronistic application of modern redaction critical studies to ancient texts, see J. Van Seters, "The Redactor in Biblical Studies: A Nineteenth Century Anachronism," *Journal of Northwest Semitic Languages* 29 (2003): 1–19. See also J. Van Seters, "An Ironic Circle: Wellhausen and the Rise of Redaction Criticism," *Zeitschrift für die Alttestamentliche Wissenschaft* 115 (2003): 487–500.

23. M. C. Amodio, *Writing the Oral Tradition: Oral Poetics and Literate Culture in Medieval England* (Notre Dame, IN: University of Notre Dame Press, 2004), 5.

Chapter 8 Superfluous and Self-Incriminating Testimony

1. For a more comprehensive look at these two questions, see the relevant sections in chapter 10 of Eddy and Boyd, *Jesus Legend*.

2. Each in their own way, a variety of small-scale studies have demonstrated the historical value of various details in the Gospel tradition. See, e.g., D. L. Bock, "Jewish Expressions in Mark 14.61–62 and the Authenticity of the Jewish Examination of Jesus," *Journal for the Study of the Historical Jesus* 1 (2003): 147–59; G. Theissen, *The Gospels in Context: Social and Political History in the Synoptic Tradition*, trans. L. M. Maloney (1989; repr., Minneapolis: Fortress, 1991).

3. W. Schadewaldt, "The Reliability of the Synoptic Tradition," in M. Hengel, *Studies in the Gospel of Mark*, trans. J. Bowden (Philadelphia: Fortress, 1985), 102.

4. P. Merkley, "The Gospels as Historical Testimony," *Evangelical Quarterly* 58 (1986): 335–36. Referring to E. Auerbach, *Mimesis: The Representation of Reality in Western Literature*, trans. W. Trask (Garden City, NY: Doubleday, 1957).

5. See M. K. Johnson and C. L. Raye, "Reality Monitoring," *Psychological Review* 88 (1981): 67–85.

6. Ibid., 71.

7. Schadewaldt, "Reliability of the Synoptic Tradition," in Hengel, *Studies in the Gospel of Mark*, 102.

8. E.g., *bar* (Matt. 16:17), *talitha cum* (Mark 5:41), *ephphatha* (Mark 7:34), *golgotha* (Mark 15:22).

9. J. Jeremias, *The Problem of the Historical Jesus*, trans. N. Perrin (Philadelphia: Fortress, 1964), 18.

10. On Aramaisms and a likely Aramaic substratum for the Gospel tradition, see M. Black, *An Aramaic Approach to the Gospels and Acts*, 2nd ed. (1946; repr., Oxford: Clarendon, 1954), especially 50–185; Casey, *Aramaic Sources of Mark's Gospel*; J. Jeremias, *New Testament Theology: The Proclamation of Jesus*, trans. J. Bowden (New York: Scribner, 1971), 3–37. One does not have to agree with any author's particular thesis about the extent of an (oral or written) Aramaic substratum to appreciate the presence of Aramaisms in the Gospels and early Jesus tradition.

11. Bauckham, "Eyewitnesses and the Gospel Tradition," 28–60.

12. Ibid., 47.

13. For a detailed chart of this data, see ibid., 44–46.

14. Ibid., 49.

15. Eusebius, *Church History*, 3.11; 4.22.4.

16. It is significant that Mark assumed his audience knew who Alexander and Rufus were (he mentions them only to explain who Simon of Cyrene was). This suggests Mark was writing within one or two generations of the events he records. The sons of the very man who helped Jesus carry the cross were familiar to his audience, which means they were either still alive or quite recently deceased.

17. Bauckham, "Eyewitnesses and the Gospel Tradition," 55.

18. John Meier lists the criterion of embarrassment among what he considers to be the five primary criteria of historicity; Meier, *Marginal Jew*, vol. 1, 168–71.

19. Given the oral register of these texts, we think it more likely that this softening occurred over the process of oral transmission than it is that the authors—in a moment of unconventional redactional brilliance—intentionally modified the tradition.

20. For discussions, see Witherington, *Christology of Jesus*, 4; C. Blomberg, "Form Criticism," in *Dictionary of Jesus and the Gospels*, ed. Green, McKnight, and Marshall, 246.

Chapter 9 How Am I Supposed to Believe *That*?

1. For a more comprehensive look at these two questions, see the relevant sections in chapter 10 of Eddy and Boyd, *Jesus Legend*.

2. See, for example, C. Blomberg, *The Historical Reliability of the Gospels* (Downers Grove, IL: InterVarsity, 1987), 113–52; S. L. Bridge, *Getting the Gospels: Understanding the New Testament Accounts of Jesus' Life*

(Peabody, MA: Hendrickson, 2004); and R. H. Stein, *Interpreting Puzzling Texts in the New Testament* (Grand Rapids: Baker, 1996), parts 1–2.

3. See R. M. Grant, *The Earliest Lives of Jesus* (New York: Harper, 1961).

4. G. Garraghan, *A Guide to Historical Method* (New York: Fordham, 1946), 314. See also J. Topolski, *Methodology of History* (Warsaw: PWN—Polish Scientific Publishers, 1976), 471–73.

5. J. Cameron, interview for "Titanic: Breaking New Ground," a televised documentary, aired on March 24, 1998.

6. Foley, *Immanent Art*, 7.

7. R. Thomas, *Literacy and Orality in Ancient Greece* (New York: Cambridge University Press, 1992), 76–77.

8. Ibid., 76, emphasis added.

9. T. M. Lentz, *Orality and Literacy in Hellenic Culture* (Carbondale, IL: Southern Illinois University Press, 1989), 92, emphasis added. See also F. A. Yates, *The Art of Memory* (Chicago: University of Chicago Press, 1966), 29–31.

10. A point Augustine recognized in his harmony long ago; see Stein, *Interpreting Puzzling Texts*, 26–28. It is also possible that this apparent contradiction involves separate traditions of Jesus giving different instructions to his missionaries at different points in his ministry.

11. For a clear explication of this phenomenon drawn from contemporary Malay culture, see A. Sweeney, *A Full Hearing: Orality and Literacy in the Malay World* (Berkeley: University of California Press, 1987), esp. 8–12, 272, 297–98, 305.

12. S. A. Sowayan, *The Arabian Oral Historical Narrative: An Ethnographic and Linguistic Analysis* (Wiesbaden, Germany: Harrassowitz, 1992), 19.

13. Ibid., 22.

14. Ibid., 23.

15. See, e.g., Robin Law, "How Truly Traditional Is Our Traditional History? The Case of Samuel Johnson and the Recording

of Yoruba Oral Tradition," *History in Africa* 11 (1984): 198.

16. A point forcefully made by Wright, *Jesus and the Victory of God*, 170–71.

17. W. Kelber, "Jesus and Tradition: Words in Time, Words in Space," *Semeia* 65 (1994): 146.

18. Wright, *Jesus and the Victory of God*, 170.

19. Ibid., 170; see also 632–33.

20. Ibid., 171.

21. See B. Allen and W. L. Montell, *From Memory to History: Using Oral Sources in Local Historical Research* (Nashville: American Association for State and Local History, 1981), 79. They offer as one historical test "whether or not the information provided in a given text is logical." They never explore the complex problem of *whose logic* is allowed to pass judgment on whose.

Chapter 10 Jesus and Ancient Non-Christian Writers

1. For a more comprehensive look at the question of external literary evidence for Jesus, see Eddy and Boyd, *Jesus Legend*, chapter 4.

2. Julius Africanus, cited in M. Harris, "References to Jesus in Classical Authors," in *Jesus Traditions Outside the Gospels*, ed. D. Wenham (Sheffield, UK: Sheffield Academic Press, 1982), 343.

3. G. A. Wells, *The Jesus Myth* (LaSalle, IL: Open Court, 1999), 285n1; Doherty, *Jesus Puzzle*, 203.

4. Pliny, book 10, letter 96, as cited in C. A. Evans, "Jesus in Non-Christian Sources," in *Studying the Historical Jesus: Evaluations of the State of Current Research*, ed. B. Chilton and C. A. Evans (New York: Brill, 1994), 459.

5. As cited in R. E. Van Voorst, *Jesus Outside the New Testament: An Introduction to the Ancient Evidence* (Grand Rapids: Eerdmans, 2000), 30.

6. Ibid., 33.

7. Among scholars who conclude that it is likely Suetonius is referring to Jesus, see Evans, "Jesus in Non-Christian Sources," 457–58; Harris, "References to Jesus," 353–54; Meier, *Marginal Jew*, vol. 1, 92; Van Voorst, *Jesus Outside the New Testament*, 29–39.

8. While the work is lost, Origen preserved vast portions of it in his rebuttal, *Against Celsus*.

9. Lucian, "The Passing of Peregrinus," in *Lucian*, vol. 5, trans. A. M. Harmon, Loeb Classical Library (Cambridge: Harvard University Press, 1936), 13.

10. Evans, "Jesus in Non-Christian Sources," 462.

11. As cited in Evans, "Jesus in Non-Christian Sources," 464–65.

12. Meier, *Marginal Jew*, vol. 1, 91. The "vice" of Christians Tacitus refers to was most likely their lack of patriotism—refusing to honor the emperor, refusing to worship the national gods, and refusing to participate in Roman festivities or the military.

13. See, e.g., A. Drews, *The Christ Myth*, 3rd ed., trans. C. D. Burns (1810; repr., Amherst, NY: Prometheus, 1998).

14. Meier, *Marginal Jew*, vol. 1, 90; see also Evans, "Jesus in Non-Christian Sources," 465.

15. The correct title was derived from the so-called Pilate stone found in Caesarea Maritima in 1961. See J. D. Crossan and J. L. Reed, *Excavating Jesus: Beneath the Stones, Behind the Texts* (San Francisco: HarperSanFrancisco, 2001), 2.

16. To illustrate, Josephus refers to two different governors of Judea, Cuspius Fadus (ca. AD 44–46) and Porcius Festus (ca. AD 59–61) by both terms at different places (for Fadus see *Antiquities*, 19.363 and 20.2, 14; for Festus see *Antiquities*, 20.193, and *Jewish War*, 2.271). In fact, "procurator" predominates in Josephus. For discussion, see Harris, "References to Jesus," 349–50, 364n31.

17. There is virtually unanimous agreement that, by any ancient standards, Tacitus

was a very careful historian. See A. Momigliano, *The Classical Foundations of Modern Historiography* (Berkeley: University of California Press, 1990), 111–12; R. Mellor, *Tacitus* (New York: Routledge, 1993), 40; R. Syme, *Tacitus*, vol. 1 (Oxford, UK: Clarendon, 1958), 281, 398.

18. Josephus, *The Works of Josephus*, trans. W. Whiston (Peabody, MA: Hendrickson, 1987), 537–38.

19. This argument is offered by, e.g., Doherty, *Jesus Puzzle*, 216.

20. G. Twelftree, "Jesus in Jewish Traditions," in *Jesus Traditions Outside the Gospels*, ed. Wenham, 300.

21. Evans, "Jesus in Non-Christian Sources," 469.

22. Meier, *Marginal Jew*, vol. 1, 57.

23. E.g., as in Gal. 1:19 and in Hegesippus, a second-century Christian historian cited in Eusebius, *Ecclesiastical History*, 2.23.4; see also 1 Cor. 9:5—"brothers of the Lord."

24. Meier, *Marginal Jew*, vol. 1, 59.

25. For discussion, see ibid., 58.

26. Josephus, *Antiquities*, trans. L. H. Feldman (Cambridge: Harvard University Press, 1965), 48, 50.

27. This seems to be the most common reconstruction. See, e.g., J. Klausner, *Jesus of Nazareth: His Life, Times, and Teaching*, trans. H. Danby (New York: Macmillan, 1925), 55; Meier, *Marginal Jew*, vol. 1, 61.

28. See S. Pines, *An Arabic Version of the Testimonium Flavianum and Its Implications* (Jerusalem: Israel Academy of Sciences and Humanities, 1971).

29. J. H. Charlesworth, *Jesus Within Judaism* (New York: Doubleday, 1988), 96.

30. Meier, *Marginal Jew*, vol. 1, 65.

31. Some have proposed that the original passage contained even more negative elements, which have been excised by the Christian interpolator. See F. F. Bruce, *Jesus and Christian Origins Outside the New Testament* (Grand Rapids: Eerdmans, 1974), 38–40; Van Voorst, *Jesus Outside the New Testament*, 94–95.

32. Meier, *Marginal Jew*, vol. 1, 66.

33. Evans, "Jesus in Non-Christian Sources," 470.

34. L. H. Feldman, "The *Testimonium Flavianum*: The State of the Question," in *Christological Perspectives: Essays in Honor of Harvey K. McArthur*, ed. R. F. Berkey and S. A. Edwards (New York: Pilgrim, 1982), 183. A. Whealey agrees; see A. Whealey, *Josephus on Jesus: The Testimonium Flavianum Controversy from Late Antiquity to Modern Times* (New York: Lang, 2003), 13.

35. Charlesworth, *Jesus within Judaism*, 96.

36. So argues Louis Feldman in "Introduction," in *Josephus, Judaism, and Christianity*, ed. L. Feldman and G. Hata (Detroit: Wayne State University Press, 1987), 56.

37. Meier, *Marginal Jew*, vol. 1, 66.

Chapter 11 Excavating Jesus

1. For a more comprehensive look at this issue, see the relevant section in chapter 10 of Eddy and Boyd, *Jesus Legend*.

2. Some scholars argue that the Gospels, particularly Mark, contain clear examples of geographical errors. For an examination and rebuttal of this claim, see Eddy and Boyd, *Jesus Legend*, 447–51.

3. For brief summaries of the excavations of Bethsaida and Khirbet Cana, see J. H. Charlesworth, "Jesus Research and Near Eastern Archaeology: Reflections on Recent Developments," in *Neotestamentica et Philonica: Studies in Honor of Peder Borgen*, ed. D. E. Aune, T. Seland, and J. H. Ulrichsen (Boston: Brill, 2003), 55–57; and R. R. Rousseau, "The Impact of the Bethsaida Finds on Our Knowledge of the Historical Jesus," in *Society of Biblical Literature Seminar Papers 1995*, ed. E. H. Lovering (Atlanta: Scholars Press, 1995), 187–207.

4. See Rousseau, "Impact of the Bethsaida Finds," 204.

5. Crossan and Reed, *Excavating Jesus*, 3. See also S. Wachsmann, "The Galilee Boat," in *Archaeology and the Bible: The Best of BAR*,

vol. 2, *Archaeology in the World of Herod, Jesus, and Paul*, ed. H. Shanks and D. P. Cole (Washington, DC: Biblical Archaeological Society, 1990), 208–23; and J. H. Charlesworth, "Archaeological Research and Biblical Theology," in *Geschichte— Tradition—Reflexion: Festschrift für Martin Hengel zum 70. Geburtstag*, vol. 1, ed. H. Cancik, H. Lichtenberger, and P. Schäfer (Tübingen, Germany: Mohr-Siebeck, 1996), 12.

6. We are not, of course, suggesting this is the actual boat used by Jesus and his disciples. Rather this boat shows us what first-century Galilean boats were like—and it fits the description given in the Gospels nicely.

7. See Crossan and Reed, *Excavating Jesus*, 2.

8. See J. J. Rousseau and R. Arav, *Jesus and His World* (Minneapolis: Fortress, 1995), 227.

9. See J. D. Crossan, *Who Killed Jesus? Exposing the Roots of Anti-Semitism in the Gospel Story of the Death of Jesus* (San Francisco: HarperSanFrancisco, 1995), 163–68. For a case against Crossan's thesis that the burial of Jesus in a private tomb was a fabrication of the early church, see P. R. Eddy, "Response" [to W. L. Craig's "John Dominic Crossan on the Resurrection of Jesus"], in *The Resurrection: An Interdisciplinary Symposium on the Resurrection of Jesus*, ed. S. T. Davis, D. Kendall, and G. O'Collins (New York: Oxford University Press, 1997), 277–80; and Boyd, *Cynic Sage or Son of God?* chapter 13.

10. For a list of some of these archaeologists, see C. A. Evans, *Jesus and the Ossuaries* (Waco: Baylor University Press, 2003), 107.

11. This quote from an interview with J. H. Charlesworth comes from an online news story, http://www.post-gazette.com/pg/05221/550792.stm (accessed August 15, 2006). On the pool of Siloam, see H. Shanks, "The Siloam Pool," *Biblical Archaeology Review* 31, no. 5 (September–October 2005): 16–23.

12. U. C. von Wahlde, "Archaeology and John's Gospel," in *Jesus and Archaeology*, ed. J. H. Charlesworth (Grand Rapids: Eerdmans, 2006), 583.

13. See, for example, J. Murphy-O'Conner, *The Holy Land*, 4th ed. (New York: Oxford University Press, 1998), 220. Crossan and Reed rank the locating of Peter's house as third among their "top ten archaeological discoveries" pertaining to Jesus; Crossan and Reed, *Excavating Jesus*, 2–3. See also J. F. Strange and H. Shanks, "Has the House Where Jesus Stayed in Capernaum Been Found?" in *Archaeology in the World of Herod, Jesus, and Paul*, ed. Shanks and Cole, 188–99; and Charlesworth, "Jesus Research," 61–62.

14. See Charlesworth, "Jesus Research," 51; D. Bahat, "Does the Holy Sepulchre Church Mark the Burial of Jesus?" in *Archaeology in the World of Herod, Jesus, and Paul*, ed. Shanks and Cole, 248–66; M. Broshi, "Evidence of Earliest Christian Pilgrimage to the Holy Sepulchre Comes to Light in Holy Sepulchre Church," in *Archaeology in the World of Herod, Jesus, and Paul*, ed. Shanks and Cole, 267–69; Crossan and Reed, *Excavating Jesus*, 248–49.

15. See E. M. Yamauchi, *The Stones and the Scriptures* (Philadelphia: Lippincott, 1972), 99. Though it lies outside the consideration of this book, we should mention that the archaeological confirmation of Acts is, in our estimation, noteworthy. See Hemer, *Book of Acts in the Setting of Hellenistic History*; and Craig Keener's forthcoming commentary on Acts to be published by Eerdmans. For a summary of some of the more impressive evidence, see Boyd, *Cynic Sage or Son of God?* chapter 12.

16. For the case that Luke is saying that the census that led Joseph and Mary to Bethlehem took place *before* the census taken under Quirinius, see B. W. R. Pearson, "The Lucan Censuses, Revisited," *Catholic Biblical Quarterly* 61 (1999): 262–82.

17. See J. McRay, *Archaeology and the New Testament* (Grand Rapids: Baker, 1990), 154.

18. H. Shanks and B. Witherington, *The Brother of Jesus: The Dramatic Story and Meaning of the First Archaeological Link to Jesus and His Family* (San Francisco: HarperSanFrancisco, 2003).

19. A. Lemaire, "The Burial Box of James the Brother of Jesus," *Biblical Archaeology Review* (November/December 2002): 33.

20. Lemaire, "Burial Box of James," 29.

21. See H. Shanks, "The Storm Over the Bone Box: Ossuary Update," *Biblical Archaeological Review* (September/October 2003): 30.

22. For the full text of Krumbein's report see http://www.bib-arch.org/bswbOO-ossuary_Krumbeinreport.pdf (accessed August 15, 2006). For a summary version that includes the quote in the text above see http://www.bib-arch.org/bswbOOossuary_Krumbeinsummary.asp (accessed August 15, 2006).

23. For a balanced and evenhanded overview, see Evans, *Jesus and the Ossuaries*, 112–22.

24. So argues J. Magness, "Ossuaries and the Burials of Jesus and James," *Journal of Biblical Literature* 124 (2005): 154.

25. Lemaire, "Burial Box of James," 33.

Chapter 12 Myth Incarnate

1. J. Campbell, *The Inner Reaches of Outer Space: Metaphor as Myth and Religion* (New York: van der Marck, 1986), 55.

2. See, for example, D. Richardson, *Eternity in Their Hearts*, rev. ed. (1981; repr., Ventura, CA: Regal, 1984); D. Richardson, *Peace Child*, 3rd ed. (1974; repr., Glendale, CA: Regal, 1976).

3. C. S. Lewis, "Is Theology Poetry?" in *The Weight of Glory, and Other Addresses*, rev. ed. (1949; New York: Macmillan, 1980), 128.

4. Ibid., 128–29.

5. Ibid., 129–30. See also C. S. Lewis, "Myth Became Fact," in *God in the Dock: Essays on Theology and Ethics*, ed. W. Hooper (Grand Rapids: Eerdmans, 1970), 63–67.

6. J. R. R. Tolkien, "On Fairy-Stories," in *Leaf and Tree* (Boston: Houghton Mifflin, 1965), 71–72.

7. Ibid.

8. Ibid.

9. Ibid.

10. Freud's thesis is presented in Sigmund Freud, *The Future of an Illusion*, trans. J. Strachey (New York: Norton, 1976).

11. Augustine, *Confessions*, bk. 1, chap. 1.

Index of Scripture and Ancient Writings

General Index

Gregory A. Boyd (PhD, Princeton Theological Seminary) is senior pastor of Woodland Hills Church in St. Paul, Minnesota. He is the author or coauthor of more than fifteen books, including *The Jesus Legend, Cynic Sage or Son of God?* and ECPA Gold Medallion Award–winner *Letters from a Skeptic.*

Paul Rhodes Eddy (PhD, Marquette University) is professor of biblical and systematic theology at Bethel University in St. Paul, Minnesota. He is author, coauthor, or coeditor of eight books, including *The Jesus Legend, The Nature of the Atonement*, and *John Hick's Pluralist Philosophy of World Religions.*